George B. Kulp

Historical Essays

Indians. Teedyuscung. Old Forge. early methodism. coal; its antiquity.

sabbath--Sunday

George B. Kulp

Historical Essays

Indians. Teedyuscung. Old Forge. early methodism. coal; its antiquity. sabbath--Sunday

ISBN/EAN: 9783337066475

Printed in Europe, USA, Canada, Australia, Japan

Cover: Foto ©ninafisch / pixelio.de

More available books at **www.hansebooks.com**

HISTORICAL ESSAYS.

INDIANS. TEEDYUSCUNG.

FIRST SETTLEMENT OF WILKES-BARRE.

OLD FORGE. EARLY METHODISM.

COAL; ITS ANTIQUITY.

DISCOVERY AND EARLY DEVELOPMENT IN THE WYOMING VALLEY.

SABBATH—SUNDAY.

SUNDAY LEGISLATION.

BY

GEO. B. KULP,

HISTORIOGRAPHER OF THE WYOMING HISTORICAL AND GEOLOGICAL SOCIETY.
AUTHOR OF "FAMILIES OF THE WYOMING VALLEY," ETC.

WILKES-BARRE, PA.
1892.

CONTENTS.

	PAGE.
INDIANS,	1
COAL,	57
SABBATH—SUNDAY,	91
OLD FORGE,	145

INDIANS.

TEEDYUSCUNG.

FIRST SETTLEMENT OF WILKES-BARRE.

TEEDYUSCUNG

INDIANS.

TEEDYUSCUNG.

FIRST SETTLEMENT OF WILKES-BARRE.

> "Alas! for them their day is o'er,
> Their fires are out from shore to shore.
> No more for them the wild deer bounds,
> The plough is on their hunting grounds;
> The pale man's axe rings through their woods,
> The pale man's sail skims o'er their floods;
> Their children—look, by power oppressed,
> Beyond the mountains of the West—
> Their children go—to die."

When the Europeans first discovered the Western Continent they found it inhabited by human beings. They called them INDIANS, because they thought they had arrived at the eastern coast of India—that great country for which they had so anxiously sought a short passage. Though erroneously applied the name then given them remains unchanged. All Europeans had been taught to call them by this name; they recognized them by it, and they could not change it. It is not known that a change of name was even suggested, much less attempted, and it is possible that these Indians received the right name by accident, though their discoverers found them in a great country, far removed from the continent, whence it is believed they had their origin. The Europeans found tribes of these Indians scattered along the entire eastern coast of this country, from Maine to Florida, and each tribe had a different name. Their origin was not then known; and it is not known now to a certainty, though four hundred years have elapsed since their discovery here. Who were they? It is supposed that they originally came from the far west, even from Asia—having wandered thence in some manner, either by land or sea, toward the rising sun, to this continent. When they landed in the west, and especially when they reached the eastern coast, is still one of the great mysteries of our interesting history. It may be that they wandered eastwardly from a given point, just as the Japhetic tribe of men wandered westwardly. If the theory of the Bible is correct, all mankind must have originated from the few survivors of the great flood, who landed on Mount Ararat, in Asia. After this great event Japheth and his family and their descendants migrated to the west; Ham, his family and their descendants to the south, and Shem, his family and their descendants to the east. Accordingly, these "Indians" may have descended from Shem.

A very long period must have elapsed till they became settled along the Atlantic coast. Yet it would seem that they had reached this point before the descendants of Japheth, who, in their developments and geographical movements, proceeded in an opposite direction. This was a remarkable meeting in the history of progressive civilization. Reckoning the flood to have transpired, according to sacred history, in the year 2348, before Christ, they met after the lapse of *three thousand eight hundred and forty years!* On the one hand, the "Indians" were guided alone by the "Great Spirit," preserving naught as they went from century to century, and from one continent to the other, but their instincts, their manners, and their languages, and apparently showing no improvement in social, mental and spiritual development, without literature of any kind, excepting rude inscriptions on rocks and stones. On the other, the Europeans were guided by reason, producing one improvement after the other in every department of life, accompanied by an abiding faith in God, by Revelation, and by the Bible, and developing literature as wonderful in extent as it was superior in character. What a vast difference in mankind such a time had produced! Who can explain it? Why were they not kept equal in the progress of time? Eastwardly, though to catch, as it were, the rising sun, and, by getting into the dawning light of day, to become possessor of his Creator's excellence, the one went into barbarity and darkness; westwardly, though after the setting sun and into darkness, the other went into civilization and light. This is a contrast, indeed, wonderful to relate and truly surprising to understand! A comparison of the manners and customs of the "Indians," as they have been given to us by early settlers and historians from the time of the first settlements in our country, say about 1600, A. D., with the manners and customs of western Asia, as they have been transmitted to us by literature for an equal period before Christ, say 1600, reveals many similarities, especially in the daily affairs of domestic life. In spiritual life both believed in God, and knew what it was to be truthful and honorable in social and political life. Yet, of the two classes which has distinguished itself the most in point of social honor and political integrity. The Indians have been universally praised for these qualities, notwithstanding their heartless barbarity and mental darkness, but the Europeans have received continuous and general condemnation for the remarkable want of these qualities, guided, even as they claimed to have been by the love of God and the light of the mind.

The Lenni Lenape, or the original people, as they called themselves, inhabited principally the shores of the river Delaware, thence their name. The Lenape were of western origin, and nearly forty tribes, according to Heckewelder, acknowledged them as their "grandfathers" or parent stock. It was related by the braves of the Delawares, that many centuries previous their ancestors dwelt far in the western wilds of the American continent, but emigrating eastwardly, arrived after many years on the Mississippi, or river of fish, where they fell in with the Mengwe (Iroquois), who had also emigrated from a distant country, and approached this river somewhat nearer its source. The spies of the Lenape reported the country on the east of the Mississippi to be inhabited by a powerful nation, dwelling in large towns erected upon their principal rivers. This people, tall and stout, some of whom, as tradition reports, were of gigantic mould, bore the name of Allegewi, and from them were derived the names of the Allegheny river and mountains. Their towns were defended by regular fortifications or intrenchments of earth, vestiges of which are yet shown in greater or less preservation. The Lenape requested permission to establish themselves in their vicinity. This was refused, but leave was given them to pass the river and seek a country farther to the eastward. But, whilst the Lenape were crossing the river, the Allegewi, becoming alarmed at their number, assailed and destroyed many of those who had reached the eastern shore, and threatened a like fate to the others should they attempt the stream. Fired at the loss they had sustained, the Lenape eagerly accepted a proposition from the Mengwe, who had hitherto been spectators only of their enterprise, to conquer and divide the country. A war of many years duration was waged by the united nations, marked by great havoc on both sides, which eventuated in the conquest and expulsion of the Allegewi, who fled by the way of the Mississippi never to return. Their devastated country was apportioned among the conquerors; the Iroquois choosing their residence in the neighborhood of the great lakes, and the Lenape possessing themselves of the lands to the south. After many ages, during which the conquerors lived together in great harmony, the enterprising hunters of the

Lenape crossed the Allegheny mountains, and discovered the great rivers Susquehanna and Delaware, and their respective bays. Exploring the *Sheyichbi* country (New Jersey) they arrived on the Hudson, to which they subsequently gave the name of the *Mohicannittuck* river. Returning to their nation, after a long absence, they reported their discoveries, describing the country they had visited as abounding in game and fruits, fish and fowl, and destitute of inhabitants. Concluding this to be the country destined for them by the Great Spirit, the Lenape proceeded to establish themselves upon the principal rivers of the east, making the Delaware, to which they gave the name of *Lenape-wihittuck* (the river or stream of the Lenape), the centre of their possessions. They say, however, that all of their nation who crossed the Mississippi did not reach this country, a part remaining behind to assist that portion of their people who, frightened by the reception which the Allegewi had given to their countrymen, fled far to the west of the Mississippi. They were finally divided into three great bodies, the larger half of the whole settled on the Atlantic, the other half was separated into two parts, the stronger continued beyond the Mississippi, the other remained on its eastern bank. Those on the Atlantic were subdivided into three tribes—the Turtle or Delawares of the sea shore; the Turkeys or Delawares of the woods, and the Wolves or Delawares of the mountains. The two former inhabited the coast, from the Hudson to the Potomac, settling in small bodies in towns and villages upon the larger streams, under the chiefs subordinate to the great council of the nation. The Wolves or Minsi, called by the English Monseys, the most warlike of the three tribes, dwelt in the interior, forming a barrier between their nation and the Mengwe. They extended themselves from the Minisink on the Delaware, where they held their council seat, to the Hudson on the east, to the Susquehanna on the southwest, to the head waters of the Delaware and Susquehanna rivers on the north, and to that range of hills now known in New Jersey by the name of Muskenecun, and by those of Lehigh and Conewago in Pennsylvania. Many subordinate tribes proceeded from these, who received names from their places of residence, or from some accidental circumstance, at the time of its occurrence remarkable, but now forgotten. Such probably were the Shawanese, the Nanticokes, the Susquehannas, the Neshamines, and other tribes resident in or near the province of Pennsylvania at the time of its settlement. The Mengwe hovered for some time on the border of the lakes, with their canoes in readiness to fly should the Allegewi return. Having grown bolder, and their numbers increasing, they stretched themselves along the St. Lawrence, and became, on the north, near neighbors to the Lenape tribes. The Mengwe and the Lenape in the progress of time became enemies. The latter represent the former as treacherous and cruel, pursuing pertinaciously an insiduous and destructive policy toward their more generous neighbors. Dreading the power of the Lenape, the Mengwe resolved to involve them in war with distant tribes, to reduce their strength. They committed murders upon the members of one tribe, and induced the injured party to believe they were perpetrated by another. They stole into the country of the Delawares, surprised them in their hunting parties, slaughtered the hunters and escaped with the plunder. Each nation or tribe had a particular mark upon its war clubs which, left beside a murdered person, denoted the aggressor. The Mengwe perpetrated a murder in the Cherokee country, and left with the dead body a war club bearing the insignia of the Lenape. The Cherokees, in revenge, fell suddenly upon the latter and commenced a long and bloody war. The treachery of the Mengwe was at length discovered, and the Delawares turned upon them with the determination utterly to extirpate them.

They were the more strongly induced to take this resolution, as the cannibal propensities of the Mengwe, according to Heckewelder, had reduced them, in the estimation of the Delawares, below the rank of human beings. Hitherto each tribe of the Mengwe had acted under the direction of its particular chiefs, and, although the nation could not control the conduct of its members, it was made responsible for their outrages. Pressed by the Lenape, they resolved to form a confederation which might enable them better to concentrate their force in war, and to regulate their affairs in peace. Thannawage, an aged Mohawk, was the projector of this alliance. Under his auspices, five nations—the Mohawks, Oneidas, Onondagoes, Cayugas and Senecas formed a species of republic, governed by the united councils of their aged and experienced chiefs. To these a sixth nation, the Tuscaroras, was added in 1712. This last originally dwelt in the western parts of North Carolina, but having formed a deep and general conspiracy to exterminate the whites, were, as stated in Smith's history of New York, driven from their country and adopted by the Iroquois confederacy. The beneficial effects of this system early displayed themselves. The Lenape were checked, and the Mengwe, whose warlike disposition soon familiarized them with fire arms procured from the Dutch, were enabled, at the same time, to contend with them and to resist the French, who now attempted the settlement of Canada, and to extend their conquests over a large portion of the country between the Atlantic and Mississippi. But, being pressed hard by their new enemies, they became desirous of reconcilliation with their old enemies, and for this purpose, if the tradition of the Delawares be credited, they effected one of the most extraordinary strokes of policy which history has recorded. The mediators between the Indian nations at war are the women. The men, however weary of the contest, hold it cowardly and disgraceful to seek reconcilliation. They deem it inconsistent in a warrior to speak of peace with bloody weapons in his hands. He must maintain a determined courage, and appear at all times as ready and willing to fight as at the commencement of hostilities. With such dispositions, Indian wars would be interminable if the women did not interfere and persuade the combatants to bury the hatchet and make peace with each other. On these occasions the women pleaded their cause with much eloquence. "Not a warrior," they would say, "but laments the loss of a son, a brother or a friend. And mothers, who have borne with cheerfulness the pangs of child-birth, and the anxieties that wait upon the infancy and adolescence of their sons, behold their promised blessings crushed in the field of battle, or perishing at the stake in unutterable torments. In the depth of their grief they curse their wretched existence, and shudder at the idea of bearing children." They conjured the warriors, therefore, by their suffering wives, their helpless children, their homes and their friends, to interchange forgiveness, to cast away their arms, and smoking together the pipe of amity and peace, to embrace as friends those whom they had learned to esteem as enemies. Prayers thus urged seldom failed of their desired effect. The function of the peace-maker was honorable and dignified, and its assumption by a courageous and powerful nation could not be inglorious. This station the Mengwe urged upon the Lenape. "They had reflected," they said, "upon the state of the Indian race and were convinced that no means remained to preserve it unless some magnanimous nation would assume the character of the *woman*. It could not be given to a weak and contemptible tribe, such would not be listened to, but the Lenape and their allies would at once possess influence and command respect." The facts upon which these arguments were founded were known to the Delawares, and, in a moment of blind confidence in the sincerity of the Iroquois, they acceded to the proposition and assumed the petticoat. The ceremony of the metamorphosis was performed with great rejoicings at Albany, in 1617, in the presence of the Dutch, whom the Lenape charged with having conspired with the Mengwe for their destruction. Having thus disarmed the Delawares, the Iroquois assumed over them the rights of protection and command. But still dreading their strength, they artfully involved them again in war with the Cherokees, promised to fight their battles, led them into an ambush of their foes, and deserted them. The Delawares at length comprehended the treachery of their arch enemy, and resolved to resume their arms, and being still superior in numbers, to crush them. But it was too late. The Europeans were now making their way into the country in every direction, and gave ample employment to the astonished Lenape. The Mengwe denied these machinations. They averred that they conquered the Delawares by force of arms, and made them a subject people. And, though it was said they were unable to detail the circumstances of this conquest, it is more rational to suppose it true, than that a brave, numerous and warlike nation should have voluntarily suffered themselves to be disarmed and enslaved by a shallow artifice, or, that discovering the fraud practiced upon them, they should unresistingly have submitted to its consequences. This conquest was not an empty acquisition to the Mengwe. They claimed dominion over all the lands occupied by the Delawares, and, in many instances, their claims were distinctly acknowledged. Parties of the Five Nations occasionally occupied the Lenape country and wandered over it at all times at their pleasure. Eventually, in 1756, Teedyuscung, the noted Delaware chief, seems to have compelled the Iroquois to acknowledge the independence of his tribe, but the claim of superiority was often afterwards revived.

Teedyuscung, according to his own statement, was born about the year 1700, in New Jersey, east of Trenton, in which neighborhood his ancestors of the Lenape had been seated from time immemorial. Old Captain Harris, a noted Delaware, was the father of Teedyuscung. The same was the father also of Captain John of Nazareth, of young Captain Harris, of Tom, of Joe and of Sam Evans, a family of high spirited sons who were not in good repute with their white neighbors. The latter named them, it is true, for men of their own people, and Teedyuscung they named "Honest John," yet they disliked and then feared them, for the Harrises were known to grow moody and resentful, and were heard to speak threatening words as they saw their paternal acres passing out of their hands and their hunting grounds converted into pasture and ploughed fields. These they left with reluctance and migrated westward in company with others of the Turtles or Delawares of the lowlands, some from the Raritan, some from below Cranberry and Devil's Brook, some from the Neshannock, and some from the Mouth of Squan and the meadows on Little and Great Egg Harbor. Crossing the great river of their nation they entered the province of Pennsylvania in its Forks. This was about 1730. Finding no white men here they gypsied unmolested along the Lehieton, Martin's and Cobus creeks, the Manakasy, Gattoshacki and the Hockendocque, all south and along the Aquanshicola and Pocopoco north of the Blue Mountain. On crossing this barrier they reached the land of their kinsmen, the Wolf Delawares or Monseys. By these hardy mountaineers they were kindly received, and with them they would often speak of their compulsory exodus from the east, to which the Monseys made no reply, but only smiled.

Scotch Irish immigrants began to crowd the Delawares in the Forks, south of the mountain, as early as 1735. Two years prior whites had surveyed and located unpurchased lands in the upper valley of the Delaware, thereby exasperating the Monseys and engendering in their hearts an implacable resentment which they cherished long after the Turtle Delawares had buried the hatchet and were willing to treat for redress. These highlanders were the warriors who, moody and sullen, hung back at Trout Creek in July, 1756, when Teedyuscung and his company were already in Easton engaged in negotiations for peace. In 1737 the one and a half day's walk was performed. Captain John and other Fork Indians south of the mountain were expelled from their corn lands and peach orchards in 1742. Thus wrong was being heaped on wrong against a day of retribution. Zinzendorf's reconnoisance in July of that year introduced the Moravian missionaries into the homes of the Eastern Delawares, and from that time they preached the Gospel to them on both sides of the mountain. Teedyuscung, too, heard them first on the Aquanshicola and then on the Mahoning. Impressed by the words of the plainly clad preachers from Bethlehem his religious feelings were moved, and a time came when he was convicted of sin and then sought for admission into Christian fellowship with the Mohicans and Delawares of Gnadenhutten near the mouth of Mahoning creek, Carbon county, by baptism. The brethren hesitated long before they acceded to his request, for they tell us that the man was unstable as water, and like a reed shaken before the wind. Hence they granted him a time of probation, and as he reiterated his request at its close they consented to admit him into their communion. On the twelfth of March, accordingly, he was baptized in the little turreted chapel on the Mahoning, Bishop Cammerhoff administering the rite. The ceremony was performed in accordance with the solemn ritual observed among the Moravians at that time in the baptism of adults, and when the straight limbed Delaware, robed in white, rose from bended knee, he rose as Gideon the namesake of "the son of Joash the Abiezrite, who threshed wheat in the wine press to hide it from the Midianites." Thus Teedyuscung became a member of the Christian church, and yet failed as so many do to become a Christian. The lessons of the Divine Master whom he had promised to follow proved distasteful to him as he found they demanded renunciation of self, the practice of humility, the forgiveness of injuries and the return of good for evil. They were different from the doctrines taught in the school of nature in which he had long been educated. Hence he ill-brooked the restraints imposed upon him in the "Huts of Grace," and resisted the influence of the Good Spirit that sought to dispossess him of the resentment that burned within his soul when he remembered how his countrymen were being injured by the whites and how they had been traduced and were being oppressed by the imperious Iroquois. And once when his untamed brethren came down from the Minisinks to Gnadenhutten, bringing their unshod ponies and their broken flint locks to the smithy they opened their hearts to him wide and took him into their councils. These intended war. Telling him that the hour was come to prepare to rise against their oppressors they asked him to lead them and be their king. That was the evil moment in which he was dazzled by the prospect of a crown and trafficked his peace of mind for the unrest of ambition. This was in the spring of 1754. Mohican Abraham also turned renegade, and the two chieftains together prevailed with seventy of the congregation to remove to Wyoming. The Delaware chief at Wyoming was Tadame or Tammany, of whom at this day but little is known. He was variously called Temane, Tamenand, Taminent, Tameny and Tammany. According to one account he was the first Indian to welcome William Penn to this country, and was a party to Penn's famous treaty. A tradition is that the evil spirit sought to gain a share in the administration of his kingdom, but Tammany refused to hold intercourse with him. The enemy then resorted to strategy and attempted to enter his country, but was foiled by the chief, and at length determined to destroy him. A duel was waged for many moons, during which forests were trampled under foot, which have since remained prairie lands. Finally, Tammany tripped his adversary, threw him to the ground, and would have scalped him, but the evil spirit extricated himself and escaped to Manhattan Island, where he was welcomed by the natives. Tammany appears to have been a brave and influential chieftain, and his nation reverenced his memory by bestowing his name upon those that deserved that honor. Thus when about 1776 Col. George Morgan of Princeton visited the western Indians by direction of congress, the Delawares conferred on him the name of Tammany, as the greatest mark of respect which they could show to that gentleman, who, they said, had the same address, affability and meekness as their honored chief. In the revolutionary war his enthusiastic admirers dubbed him a saint, and he was established under the name of St. Tammany, the patron saint of America. His name was inserted in some calendars and his festival celebrated on the first day of May in every year. On that day a numerous society of his votaries walked together in procession, their hats decorated with bucks tails, and proceeded to a rural place which they called the wigwam, where, after a long talk or Indian speech had been delivered and the calumet of piece and friendship had been duly smoked, they spent the day in festivity and mirth. After dinner Indian dances were performed on the green in front of the wigwam, the calumet was again smoked and the company separated. He is now chiefly known as the patron of a democratic political organization in New York city called the Tammany society. He was, however, treacherously murdered by some of the hostile Indians from the northwest, whereupon a general council of the Delawares was convened and Teedyuscung was chosen chief sachem and duly proclaimed as such. He was residing at Gnadenhutten at the time of his advancement, but immediately removed to Wyoming which then became the principal seat of the Delawares. In the summer of 1742 an Indian council was convened in Philadelphia upon the invitation of Lieutenant Governor George Thomas, at that time administering the government of the Proprietaries, as William Penn and his successors were styled. The council was numerously attended, large delegations being present from each of the Six Nations, excepting the Senecas. Of these there were but three chiefs at the council—that nation having been prevented sending a stronger deputation by reason of a famine in their country "so great that a father had been compelled to sacrifice a part of his family, even his own children for the support and preservation of himself and the other part." There seem likewise to have been no Mohawks present. But several tribes of the Delawares were represented. The chief object for the convocation of this council was "to kindle a new fire," and "strengthen the chain of friendship" with the Indians in anticipation of a war with France. Other subjects were brought before the council for consideration. Among them the governor produced a quantity of goods—being, as he remarked, a balance due the Indians for a section of the valley of the Susquehanna "on both sides of the river," which had been purchased of the Six Nations six years before. Canassatego, a celebrated Onondaga chief, who was the principal speaker on the part of the Indians during the protracted sittings of the council, recognized the sale of the land. But in the course of their discussions he took occasion to rebuke the whites for trespassing upon the unceded lands northward of the Kittatinny Hills, and also upon the Juniata. "That country," said Canassatego, "belongs to us in right of conquest, we having bought it with our blood, and taken it from our enemies in fair war." This, however, was not the principal transaction establishing the fact that the Six Nations were in the exercise of absolute power over the Delawares. On the fourth day of the council the acting Governor called the attention of the Six Nations to the conduct of "a branch of their cousins, the Delawares," in regard to a section of territory at the forks of the river which the Proprietaries had purchased of them fifty-five years before, but from which the Indians had refused to remove. The consequence had been a series of unpleasant disturbances between the white settlers and the red men, and as the latter were ever prompt in calling upon the Proprietaries to remove white intruders from their lands, the acting Governor now in turn called upon the Six Nations to remove those Indians from the land at the Forks which had been purchased and paid for in good faith such a long while ago. After three days consideration the Indians came again into council when Canassatego opened the proceedings by saying that they had carefully examined the case and "had seen with their own eyes" that their cousins had been "a very unruly people" and that they were "altogether in the wrong." They had therefore determined to remove them. Then turning to the Delawares, and holding a belt of wampum in his hand, he spoke to them as follows:

Cousins: Let this belt of wampum serve to chastise you. You ought to be taken by the hair of the head and shaken severely till you recover your senses and become sober. You don't know what ground you stand on, nor what you are doing. Our brother Onas' cause is very just and plain and his intentions are to preserve friendship. On the other hand your cause is bad, your heart far from being upright, and you are maliciously bent to break the chain of friendship with our brother Onas and his people. We have seen with our eyes a deed signed by nine of your ancestors about fifty years ago for this very land, and a release signed not many years since by some of yourselves and chiefs now living, to the number of fifteen or upward. But how came you to take upon you to sell land at all. We conquered you, we made women of you, you know you are women and can no more sell land than women. Nor is it fit you should have the power of selling lands since you would abuse it. This land that you claim has gone through your bellies; you have been furnished with clothes, meat and drink by the goods paid you for it, and now you want it again, like little children—as you are. But what makes you sell land in the dark? Did we ever receive any part of it, even the value of a pipe shank from you for it? You have told us a blind story that you sent a messenger to us to inform us of the sale, but he never came among us nor did we ever hear anything about it. This is acting in the dark and very different from the conduct our Six Nations observe in the sale of land. On such occasions they give public notice and invite all the Indians of their United Nations and give them all a share of the presents they receive for their lands. This is the behavior of the wise United Nations. But we find you are none of our blood; you act a dishonest part, not only in this, but in other matters; your ears are ever open to slanderous reports about your brethren, you receive them with as much greediness as lewd women receive the embraces of bad men. And for these reasons we charge you to remove instantly. We don't give you the liberty to think about it. You are women. Take the advice of a wise man and remove immediately. You may return to the other side of the Delaware where you came from. But we do not know whether, considering how you have demeaned yourselves, you will be permitted to live there, or whether you have not swallowed that land down your throats as well as the land on this side. We therefore assign you two places to go to, either to Wyoming or Shamokin. You may go to either of these places, and then we shall have you more under our eye and shall see how you behave. Don't deliberate but remove away and take this belt of wampum.

This speech having been translated into English and also in 'the Delaware tongue, Canassatego took another string of wampum and procceded.

Cousins: After our just reproof and absolute order to depart from the land, you are now to take notice of what we have further to say to you. This string of wampum serves to forbid you, your children and grand-children to the latest posterity, forever meddling with land affairs. Neither you nor any that shall descend from you are ever hereafter to presume to sell any land, for which purpose you are to preserve this string in memory of what your uncles have this day given you in charge. We have some other business to transact with our brethren, and therefore depart the council and consider what has been said to you.

There was no diplomatic mincing of words in the speech of the Onondaga chieftain. He spoke not only with the bluntness of unsophisticated honesty, but with the air of one having authority, nor dared the Delawares to disobey his peremptory command. They immediately left the council and soon afterwards removed from the disputed territory—some few of them to Shamokin, but the greater portion to Wyoming. The removal of the Delawares from the Forks to Wyoming was as speedy as the order to that end had been peremptory. Some years before the Wyoming Valley had been allotted by the Delawares to a strong clan of the Shawanese. These latter had planted themselves upon the flats on the west bank of the river (Plymouth), and on their arrival at the same place the Delawares selected as the site of the town they were to build the beautiful plain on the eastern side near what is now known as the slaughter houses in the lower end of this city. Here was built the town of Maugh-wau-wa-me, the original of Wyoming. Meantime the Nanticoke Indians had removed from the eastern shore of Maryland to the lower part of the Wyoming Valley, which yet retains their name. The Shawanese made no opposition to the arrival of their new neighbors. The Wanamese, under their chief, Jacob, resided on the east side of the Susquehanna above Mill Creek, known as Jacob's Plains. The Mohicans came to Wyoming with the Delawares in 1742, and under their chief, Abram, built a village above Forty Fort known as Abram's Plains. Besides these there were a few wigwams on Shickshinny and Wapwallopen creeks, and in Salem township near Beach Haven. There was also a considerable Delaware village at Nescopeck and one on the east bank of the Susquehanna about two miles above the mouth of the Lackawanna called Asserughney. There was a Shawanese village west of Ross Hill, between Plymouth and Kingston. These are all the known locations of Indian villages within the limits of Luzerne county. The French, through the influence of Catholic missionaries who are often in advance of other denominations, had secured to their interest the Shawanese, the Delawares and other Indians on the Ohio. However, Sir William Johnson had succeeded in dividing the Six Nations. The Mohawks, Oneidas and Tuscaroras remained attached to the British cause. The Onodagas, Cayugas and Senecas declared themselves neutral, nevertheless a considerable number of the two last tribes took up the hatchet with the Delawares, Shawanese and other tribes already in alliance with the French. Efforts were made by the French through the Senecas and Cayugas to induce the Susquehanna Indians to declare in favor of Onontio, the French King, as the Indians named him. Their arts and promises were crowned with success. In 1753 they succeeded in removing nearly all of the Christian Indians from Gnadenhutten to Wyoming, hoping by this to place them beyond the influence of the whites. The news of Braddock's defeat in July, 1755, spread rapidly over the country, carrying dismay to the hearts of the English settlers. The frontiers of Pennsylvania were threatened with ruin by the victorious French and their savage allies. The government of Pennsylvania did not act with the energy and promptness which the emergency demanded. No means were adopted for the protection of the frontier settlements, and murders were committed by the skulking enemy in many places in the north and west of the province. The assembly, in one of their messages, said: "What has this government done to offend the Delawares and Shawanese? Have we not always lived in peace with them? Why are they offended? Let us hold a treaty with them and persuade them." Such was the ridiculous language of the assembly when the lives of hundreds were trembling in the balance. "What has this government done to offend the Delawares?" asked the assembly. The words and deeds of Teedyuscung proclaim the deep seated offense and its cause. Sending a large belt of wampum to the Susquehanna Indians, and even to the Cherokees in the south, he said: "I am in exceeding great danger, the English will kill me, come and help me!" The Delaware town at Nescopeck was made the rendezvous of the warriors. There assembled Shingas with his western warriors, and Buchshanoath the great Shawanese war chief of Wyoming. With these Teedyuscung attacked the settlements in Berks county, November 16, 1755, spreading fire and death in all directions. On the twenty-fourth of the same month Gnadenhutten was attacked, a number of the people were murdered and the buildings were laid in ashes. It is said the murderers of the people of Gnadenhutten were commanded by a chief of the Six Nations and not by Teedyuscung. In the beginning of December of the same year a council of war was held at Wyoming by the Delawares, the Shawanese, the Nanticokes and others, at which it was determined to lay waste the whole country on the Delaware. They danced the war dance and sang their death songs. At the appointed time the paths between Wyoming and the Delaware, over which the missionaries had so often carried the white flag of peace and good will, were crowded with hostile savages on an errand of blood and death. Two hundred warriors rushed from the mountain side upon the defenceless settlements. Nearly the whole of Marshall's family, the man who performed the walk and afterwards declared that the Penns refused to pay him, were put to death. Teedyuscung, at the head of a scouting party, fired into a company assembled at a funeral. He penetrated into New Jersey and even approached within a few miles of Easton. During the month of December fifty dwelling houses were burned in Northampton county, upwards of one hundred men, women and children were murdered and scalped, and nearly as many were carried away into captivity. This destruction of life and property is attributable to the quarrel which existed between the governor and assembly in reference to taxing the proprietaries' estates. The assembly were wholly inexcusable for their neglect of the public defense at that critical period. The great body of the Indians in Pennsylvania who were disposed to arm against the French, being left to themselves and unsupported by the government, were easily persuaded by the promises and presents of the French agents to make war against the English. Paxinos, an aged Shawanese chief residing at Wilkes-Barre, was a friend of the English. It was he who, in the interview with Charles Broadhead, on November 9, 1755, at Wyoming, urged upon him to send a messenger to the Indians in the valley with belts of wampum and presents to secure them to the English interest. The message contained a warm and pressing invitation to all the Indians to attend a treaty to be held on January 1, 1756, at John Harris's. But before the messenger started on his dangerous journey Teedyuscung had devastated the country of the Delawares, and among others the plantations of Mr. Broadhead and of Aaron Dupuy, who had been selected to bear the message to the Wyoming Indians. On January 1, he was engaged with thirty of his warriors in scalping the remaining inhabitants and burning their dwellings in Smithfield township, Monroe county. To return to Paxinos. He used every argument to persuade the Delawares and his own warriors from taking up the hatchet against the English. He pressed his solicitations with such zeal that the Delawares threatened to take his life. When the warriors began to dance the war dance he, with Abram and about thirty others, chiefly old men and women, retired to a village west of Kingston, near Blindtown, where he remained until all the Indians departed the valley for the country of the Six Nations. On January 1, 1756, Buckshenoath, leading a party of savages, attacked and put to flight a company of forty soldiers at Gnadenhutten, sent to erect a fort at that place. Buckshenoath was a co-worker with Teedyuscung in his expedition against the English. At this time Teedyuscung captured Peter Hess and others. On his return to Wyoming with his booty and his prisoners he encamped for the night on the Pokono mountain. Here the savages killed Peter Hess, cutting him almost in pieces with their knives, and tied the others to trees. They kindled a large fire, but the night was so cold they could not sleep. At daylight they set out and arrived at Wyoming in the evening. They found the valley deserted. The party pushed on to Tunkhannock, where they found about one hundred men, women and children, and where the prisoners remained until the cold weather was over. They were afterwards taken to Diahoga and stayed there until they were brought down and delivered up to their friends at the treaty at Easton in the following November. In April Governor Morris, with the approval of the Supreme Executive Council, except James Logan, who entered his protest, issued a declaration of war against the Delawares and their associates, *and offered the following bounties for scalps and prisoners:* For a male Indian prisoner above twelve years of age, delivered at the government forts or towns, one hundred and fifty dollars; for every male or female prisoner twelve years old or under, one hundred and thirty dollars; for the scalp of every male Indian above twelve years old, one hundred and thirty dollars, and for the scalp of an Indian woman, fifty dollars. Through the influence of General Johnson, afterwards Sir William Johnson, with the Six Nations, the way was paved for a council with Teedyuscung. The declaration of war was suspended for thirty days, and Captain Newcastle and two other friendly Indians, in May, set out for Diahoga. Passing through Wyoming they found that the entire Indian population from Shamokin to Wyalusing had gone northward. In the valley there reigned the silence of the grave. At Diahoga, Newcastle found Teedyuscung in council with the chiefs of the Six Nations. But soon the Delawares, Shawanese, Monseys and Mohicans assembled to hear what Newcastle had to say. He delivered Governor Morris' message, inviting them to a council to be held at Easton in July. He was favorably answered by Teedyuscung and Paxinos, when he took his departure. In July, on the day appointed, Teedyuscung, with a few of his warriors, arrived in Easton, where he was met by the Governor and his councilors. The Delaware king opened the council by saying he had come as the messenger of ten nations, meaning the Six Nations, and the four who were convened to hear Newcastle at Diahoga. He wished to hear what the governor had to say. "If it be good I shall lay hold of it and carry it to the United Nations, who will smile and be pleased to hear good news, and if what you say be disagreeable, I will, notwithstanding, keep it close (closing his fist), and deliver it faithfully to the nations. Hearken to what I say. Abundance of confusion, disorder and distraction have arisen among Indians from people taking upon them to be kings and persons of authority. With every tribe of Indians there have been such pretenders, who have held treaties, sometimes public, sometimes in the bushes. Sometimes what they did was come to be known, but frequently remained in darkness. To some they held up their belts, but others never saw them. This bred among the Indians heart-burnings and quarrels, and I can assure you that the present clouds do, in a great measure, owe their rise to this wild and irregular way of doing business, and the Indians will have no more transactions in the dark." Here he presented the governor a string of wampum. Being asked if he had done speaking, he said he had for the present. The main thing he added is yet in my breast, laying his hand on his heart, but this will depend on what words the governor will speak to us. Then he repeated the Delaware word *Whishshiksy*, the same in the Mohawk as *Iago*, with great earnestness and a very pathetic tone, meaning *be strong, look about, active*. The governor then spoke: "Brother, I have heard with attention all you have said, and thank you for the openness with which you have declared your sentiments." After delivering a lengthy speech he presented many belts and assured the Indians of his desire for peace. To which Teedyuscung replied as follows: "Brother, this belt," lifting up a large string of wampum, "denotes that our uncles, the Six Nations, have lately renewed their covenant chain with us. Formerly we were accounted women and employed only in women's business, but now they have made men of us, and as such are now come to this treaty, having this authority as a man to make peace. I have it in my hand, but have not opened it, but will soon declare it to the other nations. This belt holds together ten nations. We are in the middle, between the French and English. Look at it. This belt further denotes that whoever will not comply with the terms of peace the ten nations will strike him. See the dangerous circumstances I am in—strong men on both sides; hatchets on both sides. Whoever is for peace him will I join. Brother, this is a good day. Whoever will make peace let him lay hold of this belt." Here the governor took hold of the belt and said that he was pleased with what the king had said. The figures on the belt were then explained—the

English were represented on one end, the French on the other, and the land of the Indians lay between them. Teedyuscung and his son then dined with the governor, soon after which he departed for Diahoga. Major Parsons, at this council, was requested to keep a written memoranda of the general behavior and conversation of the king, from which it would seem that the high position assumed and maintained by him in council was hardly compatible or consistent with his ordinary life. "The king and his wild company were perpetually drunk, very much on Gascoon, and at times abusive to the inhabitants, for they all spoke English, more or less. The king was full of himself, saying frequently that which side soever *he* took must stand and the other fall, repeating it with insolence that he came from the French, who had pressed him much to join them against the English, that now he was in the middle, between the French and the English, quite disengaged from both sides, and whether he joined with the English or French, he would publish it aloud to the world, that all nations might know it. * * * He is a lusty, raw-boned man, haughty and very desirous of respect and command; he can drink three quarts or a gallon of rum a day without being drunk; he was the man that persuaded the Delawares to go over to the French and then attack our frontiers, and he and those with him have been concerned in the mischief done to the inhabitants of Northampton county. Some of the Indians said that between forty and fifty of their people came to Diahoga from one of the lakes about the time they set out, in order to fall upon our inhabitants, and addressed Teedyuscung to head them, but he told them he was going to the governor of Pennsylvania to treat with him concerning a peace, which the Mohawks had advised him to do, and therefore he ordered them to sit still till he came back again to them. The townspeople observed that the shirts which the Indian women had on were made of Dutch tablecloths, which it is supposed they took from the people they murdered on our frontiers. The king, in one of his conversations, said that only two hundred French and about eighty Indians were at the lake, where most of the English are, and that he could bring the most or all of them off. The governor invited Teedyuscung and the Indians to dine with him, but before dinner the king, with some of them, came to the governor and made the governor four speeches, giving four strings of wampum, after the Indian manner; one to brush thorns from the governor's legs, another to rub the dust out of his eyes to help him see clearly, another to open his ears, and the fourth to clear his throat that he might speak plainly. Teedyuscung claimed to be king of ten nations. Being asked what ten nations, he answered, the united Six Nations—Mohawks, Onondagos, Oneidas, Senecas, Cayugas and Tuscaroras, and four others—Delawares, Shawanese, Mohicans and Munsies, who would all ratify what he should do. He carried the belt of peace with him, and whoever would might take hold of it. But as to them that refused, the rest would all join together and fall upon them. All the Indians, in short, would do as he would have them, as he was the great man. The governor used the same four ceremonies to Teedyuscung, accompanied with four strings of wampum, after which the governor and Indians went to dinner, escorted by a detachment of the First Battalion of the Pennsylvania Regiment." Conrad Weiser, the interpreter, was first introduced to Teedyuscung at this time, who, after watching his movements a single day, reported to the council "that the king and the principal Indians being all yesterday under the force of liquor, he had not been favored with so good an opportunity as he could have wished of making himself acquainted with their history, but in the main he believed Teedyuscung was well inclined; he talked in high terms of his own merit, but expressed himself a friend to this province."

Teedyuncung at this council was alleged to have been the instigator of the Indian outrages upon the whites in 1755, by sending large belts of wampum to various tribes on the war path, but the shrewd informer or negotiator, with a view of personal advantage and emolument, informed Governor Morris that as Teedyuscung had brought|on the war, he was the only person that could effect a peaceful solution of all Indian affairs. To do this "Teedyuscung must have a belt of wampum at least five or six feet long and twelve rows broad, and besides the belt, he must have twelve strings to send to the several chiefs to confirm the words that he sends." Pursuant to arrangement made before he left, Teedyuscung promised to return to another council to be held in Easton in November. He returned to Easton November 8, 1756, and brought with him four chiefs of the Six Nations, sixteen Delaware Indians, two Shawanese and six Mohicans. Imposing ceremonies, both for state and security, were kept up throughout the negotiations. At three o'clock Governor Denny marched from his lodgings to the place of conference, guarded by a party of the Royal Americans in front and on the flanks, and a detachment of Col. Weiser's Provincials in subdivisions in the rear, with colors flying, drums beating and music playing, which order was always observed in going to the place where the council was held. Teedyuscung performed the part of chief speaker on this occasion for all the tribes present, as he had done at the preceding conference. He is represented to have supported the rights and claims of the Indians in a dignified and spirited manner. If his people had cowered like cravens before the rebukes of the Six Nations in the council of 1742, their demeanor was far otherwise on this occasion. The chieftain's imposing presence, his earnestness of appeal and his impassioned oratory, as he plead the cause of the long injured Lenape evoked the admiration of his enemies themselves. He always spoke in the euphonious Delaware, employing this Castillian of the new world to utter the simple and expressive figures and tropes of the native rhetoric with which his harangues were replete, although he was conversant with the white man's speech. It would almost appear from the minutes of these conferences that the English artfully attempted to evade the point at issue and to conciliate the indignant chieftain by fair speeches and uncertain promises. The hollowness of the former he boldly exposed, and the latter he scornfully rejected, so that it was soon perceived that the Indian king was as astute and sagacious as he was unmovable in the justice of his righteous demands. On being requested by the governor to state the causes of their uneasiness and subsequent hostilities, Teedyuscung enumerated several. Among them were the abuses committed upon the Indians in the prosecution of their trade, being unjustly deprived of portions of their lands, and in the execution, long before, in New Jersey, of a Delaware chief named Wekahelah, for, as the Indians allege, accidentally killing a white man—a transaction which they said they could not forget. When the governor desired specifications of the alleged wrong, Teedyuscung replied: "The kings of England and France have settled or wrought this land so as to coop us up as if in a pen. I have not far to go for another instance. This very ground that is under me (striking it with his foot), was my land and inheritance, and is taken from me by fraud. When I say this ground, I mean all the land lying between Tohiccon creek and Wyoming, on the river Susquehanna. I have not only been served so in this government, but the same thing has been done to me as to several tracts in New Jersey, over the river." When asked what he meant by fraud, Teedyuscung replied: "Where one man had formerly liberty to purchase land, and he took the deeds from the Indians and then dies, and after his death his children forge a deed like the true one, with the same

Indian names to it, and thereby take lands from the Indians which they never sold, it is fraud. Also, when one chief has land beyond the river and another chief has land on this side, both bounded by rivers, mountains and springs which cannot be moved, and the proprietaries, ready to purchase lands, buy of one chief what belongs to another. This likewise is fraud. When I had agreed to sell certain lands to the old proprietor by the course of the river, the young proprietors came and got it run by a straight course by the compass, and by that means took in double the quantity intended to be sold. This he thought was fraud." He said the Delawares had never been satisfied with the conduct of the latter since the treaties of 1737, when their fathers sold them the lands on the Delaware. He said that although the land sold was to have gone only "*as far as a man could go in a day and a half from Nashamony creek*," yet the person who measured the ground did not *walk* but *ran*. He was, moreover, as they supposed, to follow the winding bank of the river, whereas he went in a straight line. And because the Indians had been unwilling to give up the land as far as the walk extended, the governor then having the command of the English, sent for their cousins, the Six Nations, who had always been hard masters to them, to come down and drive them from their land. When the Six Nations came down the Delawares met them at a great treaty, held at the governor's house, at Philadelphia, for the purpose of explaining why they did not give up the land, but the English made so many presents to the Six Nations that their ears were stopped. They would listen to no explanation, and Canassatego had moreover abused them and called them women. The Six Nations had, however, given to them and the Shawanese the lands upon the Susquehanna and the Juniata for hunting grounds, and had so informed the governor, but notwithstanding this the whites were allowed to go and settle upon those lands. Two years ago moreover the governor had been to Albany to buy some lands of the Six Nations, and had described their purchase by *points of compass* which the Indians did not understand, including lands both upon the Juniata and the Susquehanna, which they did not intend to sell. When all those things were known to the Indians, they declared they would no longer be friends to the English, who were trying to get all their country away from them. He, however, assured the council that they were nevertheless glad to meet their old friends, the English, again, and to smoke the pipe of peace with them. He also hoped that justice would be done to them for all the injuries they had received.

The council continued nine days, and Governor Denny appears to have conducted himself with so much tact and judgment as greatly to conciliate the good will of the Indians. By his candid and ingenious treatment of them, as some of the Mohawks afterwards expressed it, "he put his hands into Teedyuscung's bosom and was so successful as to draw out the secret which neither Sir William Johnson nor the Six Nations could do." The result was a reconciliation of the Delawares of the Susquehanna with the English, and a treaty of peace upon the basis that Teedyuscung and his people were to be allowed to remain upon the Wyoming lands, and that houses were to be built for them by the proprietaries. There were, however, several matters left unadjusted, although the governor desired that every difficulty should then be discussed and every cause of complaint, as far as he possessed the power, be removed. But Teedyuscung replied that he was not empowered at the present time to negotiate upon several of the questions of grievance that had been raised, nor were all the parties interested properly represented in the council. He therefore proposed the holding of another council in the following spring at Lancaster. This proposition was acceded to, and many Indians collected at the time and place appointed.

Sir William Johnson despatched a deputation of the Six Nations thither under the charge of Col. Croghan, the deputy superintendent of the Indians, but for some reason unexplained, neither Teedyuscung nor the Delawares from Wyoming attended the council, though of his own appointment. Col. Croghan wrote to Sir William, however, that the meeting was productive of great good in checking the war upon the frontier; and in a speech to Sir William, delivered by the Senecas in June following, they claimed the credit, by their mediation, of the partial peace that had been obtained. The conduct of Teedyuscung on that occasion was severely censured by Sir William in a speech to the Onondagos, Cayugas and Senecas, and the latter were charged by the baronet to take the subject in hand and "talk to him," and should they find him in fault "make him sensible of it." In 1757, Teedyuscung requested the Governor of Pennsylvania to so fix and define his land, around his village on the Susquehanna, that "his children can never sell or yours ever buy them," and to remain so forever. He also asked the proprietary government to assist him in building houses at Wyoming before corn-planting time. Ten log houses "twenty feet by fourteen in the clear, and one twenty-four by sixteen of squared logs and dovetailed," were built for him in 1758. These were the first dwelling houses erected in Wyoming. Other buildings were subsequently erected there. To check or crush the ambitious projects of New England men about forming a colony at Wyoming, influenced their erection by Pennsylvania quite as much as any especial regard for the Delaware sachem. One of the masons was killed and scalped by six hostile Indians while engaged in this labor. The influence of Sir William Johnson, agent for Indian affairs, was invoked to bring the Six Nations to a new congress. Neither presents nor promises were spared, and in October, 1758, there was opened at Easton, one of the most imposing assemblages ever beheld in Pennsylvania. Chiefs from the six nations were there, namely: Mohawks, Oneidas, Onondagos, Cayugas, Senecas and Tuscaroras. There were also present ambassadors from the tributary tribes of Nanticokes, Canoys, Turteloes, Chenangoes, Delawares, Unamies, Minisinks, Wapingers and Shawanese. Both the governors of Pennsylvania and New Jersey attended, with Sir William Johnson and George Croghan, sub-Indian agent, a deputation from the Provincial assembly of New Jersey, and a large concourse of eminent citizens from Philadelphia and the neighboring counties. Teedyuscung, on the way to the conference, having fallen in company with the chief who had commanded the expedition against Gnaddenhutten and Fort Allen, high words rose between them, when the king raised his tomahawk and laid the chief dead at his feet. From this moment, though vengeance might slumber, he was a doomed man, a sacrifice alike to policy and revenge. At the congress Teedyuscung, eloquent and of imposing address, took at first a decided lead in the debates. But one of the chiefs of the Six Nations, on the other hand, expressed in strong language his resentment against the British colonists who had killed and imprisoned some of his tribe, and he, as well as other chiefs of those nations, took great umbrage at the importance assumed by Teedyuscung, whom, as one of the Delawares, they considered in some degree subject to their authority. Teedyuscung, however, supported the high station which he held with dignity and firmness, and the different Indian tribes at length became reconciled to each other. The conference having continued eighteen days, and all causes of misunderstanding between the English and Indians being removed, a general peace was concluded on October 26. At this treaty the boundaries of the different purchases made from the Indians were more particularly described, and they received an additional compensation for their lands, consisting of knives, hats, caps, looking glasses, tobacco boxes, shears, gunlocks, combs, clothes, shoes, stockings, blankets, and several suits of laced clothes for their chieftains, and when the business of the treaty was completed the stores of rum were opened and distributed to the Indians, who soon exhibited a scene of brutal intoxication. Great offence, it appears, was given to the ambassadors of the Six Nations at the consequence assumed, and the forward part taken, by Teedyuscung, and yet no immediate measures were adopted to chastise his supposed contumacy. A solution of what might otherwise seem difficult, both in his more bold, independent conduct and the forbearance of the Iroquois, may be found in the fact that the power of their allies was already sensibly shaken, and Great Britain was preparing with unexampled vigor to drive the French from this continent. Fort William was taken in 1757, Louisburg surrendered to their victorious arms in the summer of 1758, and far more important to the Iroquois, as it was almost in the heart of the dominions claimed by them, the shame of Braddock's defeat was washed out, and Fort Du Quesne (afterwards named Fort Pitt) had surrendered to the English the February preceding the October of 1758, when the conferences at Easton were holden. That event was a fatal blow to the widely extended claim of power on the part of the confederacy, although the council fire at Onondago was for many years after numerously surrounded by bold and ambitious chiefs and renowned warriors. In 1753 an association of persons, principally inhabitants of Connecticut, was formed for the purpose of commencing a settlement in that portion of the Connecticut territories which lay westward of the province of New York. Agents were accordingly sent out for the purpose of exploring the country and selecting a proper district. The beautiful valley upon the Susquehanna river in which the Indians of the Delaware tribe, eleven years before, had built their town of Wyoming, attracted the attention of the agents, and as they found the Indians apparently very friendly, and a considerable portion of the valley unoccupied, except for purposes of hunting, they reported in favor of commencing their settlements at that place and of purchasing the lands of the Six Nations of Indians, residing near the great lakes, who claimed all the lands upon the Susquehanna. This report was adopted by the company, and at a general meeting of commissioners from all the English American colonies, in pursuance of his majesty's instruction, for the purpose of forming a general treaty with the Indians, it was considered that a favorable opportunity would then be presented for purchasing the Wyoming lands. When the general congress of commissioners assembled at Albany the agents appointed by the Susquehanna company attended also, and having successfully effected the objects of their negotiation, obtained from the principal chiefs of the Six Nations, on the 11th day of July, 1754, a deed of the lands on the Susquehanna, including Wyoming and the country westward to the waters of the Allegheny. In the summer of 1755 the Susquehanna company, having, in the month of May preceding, procured the consent of the legislature of Connecticut for the establishment of a settlement, and if his majesty should consent, of a separate government within the limits of their purchase, sent out a number of persons to take possession of their lands at Wyoming, but finding the Indians in a state of war with the white people, the settlement of the country was at that time deemed impracticable. Teedyuscung, in September, 1760, being in Philadelphia, had a conference with Lieutenant Governor Hamilton, in which he said: "Brother, I am ready to set out, but have heard yesterday some bad news which obliges me once more to wait on you. Yesterday I was told that some of the New England people are going on the west side of Susquehannah with intent to settle the lands at Wyomink; if this should be the case then all the pains that have been taken by this government and me will be to no purpose. It is the Indians' land and they will not suffer it to be settled. I therefore desire the governor will send a smart letter to the government where those intruding people came from, to forbid this proceeding, and tell their governor plainly that if they do not go away the Indians will turn them off;" he added with a great deal of warmth, "these people cannot pretend ignorance, and if they shall then continue on the lands it will be their own fault if anything happens," and repeated his entreaties to the governor to take every measure in his power to prevent the settlement of those lands, for it will certainly bring on another Indian war. The governor informed Teedyuscung that he had, the other day, received some information of this matter, and that as the justices of the peace were holding a court at Easton, he ordered the sheriff and some of the said justices to go to the place where it is said these New England men are settling, and if they find any people settling, to let them know they are sent by this government to warn them off, show them the bad consequences that would ensue on such an encroachment on lands belonging to the Indians and the proprietaries, and forthwith to report what they find doing, that proper measures may be taken to prevent it. Teedyuscung further desired that he might be made acquainted with whatever is doing of this sort, for if the governor can't the Indians will put a stop to it, and he was answered that he should certainly be informed of it. On April 6, 1761, Teedyuscung was again in Philadelphia with some of the Delaware and Opies Indians, and had another conference with Lieutenant Governor Hamilton. He spoke as follows: "Brother, I have, for four or five years, been constantly employed in promoting the good work of peace, and now something looks darkish, and unless what makes it look so be removed, it may be hurtful to our old men, women and children, notwithstanding all that has been done. Brother,

I never did hide anything in my heart, and I desire if the governor has anything in his heart that he would not hide it. This is the way to keep all things right between us, which cannot be done if we hide from one another what is upon our minds. Brother, you may remember that when I was here in the fall of the year I informed you that some New England people were settling the Indian lands near a place called Cushietunck, and expressed a great deal of uneasiness at it. You told me that you had likewise heard something of it, and had sent the sheriff and magistrates of the county, bordering on these lands, to the place, with orders to see what was doing, and to warn any persons off whom they should (find) settling there. You likewise said that as soon as you should be informed by these people of what they should find doing there you would send a message to the government of Connecticut to know if they were abetted by it and what were their future designs. Brother, I have not heard anything from you since that time, and our people are become so uneasy at this new settlement that several of them are moved away to other places and these now present are come on purpose with me to hear what you have to say about this affair. Brother, some of the Opies were coming to settle at Wyomink, but being disturbed at what they hear, they have sent their king that they may hear what you have to say, and know the matter from you before they proceed further. So many stories were brought to Wyomink that I, myself, was almost ready to leave my house, but I thought I would come and see you first and consult with you about it. Brother, the reason why we were so uneasy is this: About three weeks ago Robert White came to our town, along with Thomas King, one of the Six Nation Indians, and told us they had been at Cushietunck among these people, and that Sir William Johnson had sent to warn them off if they intended to settle there; if only to trade, then he desired they would use the Indians well and give them no offense. But they made very light of it, and said they would not regard either what Sir William Johnson should say, nor the governor of Pennsylvania, nor the magistrates, but only what should come from their own governor. They said they had bought that land from some Indians who were at the last treaty at Easton, and would settle there. They said likewise, that in the spring when there should be plenty of grass they would come and settle the lands at Wyomink, and that Thomas King had given leave to settle the Wyomink land, and if the Indians who lived there should hinder their settlement, they would fight it out with them and the strongest should hold the land. Robert White added that they told him that they should be four thousand strong in the spring and would all come to Wyomink. Robert White told us further that they kept continued watch for fear the Indians should shoot them." Teedyuscung being asked how many Robert White found there, he answered that Robert White told them there were thirty families. Another conference was held with the same Indians and Governor Peters on April 11. The governor acquainted Teedyuscung that he would now give him an answer to his speech, and then began as follows: "Brother, I readily acknowledge the zeal with which you have for some years past concurred with this government in promoting the good work of peace, and it is owing, in a great measure, to your endeavors that the same has been brought to an happy conclusion. Brother, you will please to observe that the people who are attempting to settle your lands, and in so doing justly give you so much uneasiness, are none of them of this province, they come from a distant government and set up pretentions for this land partly under the charter of Connecticut, the colony from whence they came, and partly under what they call Indian purchases, for besides what they told Robert White, that they had purchased that land from some Indians that were at the last treaty at Easton, they did assure the gentleman whom I sent to warn them off that they had bought it from Delaware Indians, who had signed them deeds for it, which I shall read to you that you may inquire into the truth of this matter." (He here read the names of eighteen Indians who had signed the deeds.) "Brother, you may depend upon it that this government will strictly observe their treaties with the Indians and will spare no pains to hinder these people from settling these lands. In proof of this I shall faithfully relate to you what I have done in consequence of the last conference we had together on this subject. I never did nor never will hide anything from you, being fully persuaded that openness on all occasions is the only way to confirm one another in a lasting friendship. Brother, agreeably to what I lately told you, as soon as it came to my knowledge that people were settling in the upper parts of Northampton county, beyond the bound of the lands purchased by the proprietaries of the Indians, I sent the sheriff and magistrates of that county to lay before them the dangerous consequences that might follow from such a proceeding and to desire they would desist and go away, and I was in hopes my message would have had a good effect, but when it was reported to me by those gentlemen that they said they would persist in their settlement, and that they were supported by the government of Connecticut in what they did, I immediately sent a letter to their governor, informing him of my message to these settlers and of their answer, and did not fail in the strongest terms I was able to represent to him, that such a settlement was not only against law and the rights of the proprietaries of Pennsylvania, to whom the king had granted these lands, but that you and your Indians at Wyomink had formerly complained of this settlement as a violation of your right, the lands not being purchased from the Indians, and that being done without consent of the Indians it would endanger the peace so happily concluded between them and his majesty's subjects at Easton, and I did insist that the governor of Connecticut should send for these people, put a stop to their settlement, and discountenance all such dangerous proceedings; and if, nevertheless, they should continue in their unjust attempts, they might depend upon it, that in support of the proprietary and Indian rights, I would oppose them with all my might. To this letter I have, as yet, received no answer, which keeps me in the dark, so that I know not what the intentions of the government of Connecticut are, nor what measures these people will take. At the time I wrote to Governor Fitch, I published a proclamation strictly forbidding all the inhabitants of this province from joining themselves to these intruders, and giving it in charge to all his majesty's subjects to bring any persons who shall be found settling those lands or encouraging such as did, before the proper magistrates, in order that they might be dealt with according to law. And you may assuredly rely on my carrying this proclamation into execution, and doing everything in my power to remove these unlawful intruders. But then, all this will be ineffectual, if, whilst some Indians are complaining against them, others, as they say, are encouraging them and are content to have them settle." Teedyuscung thanked the governor and expressed great satisfaction therewith. He asked what should be done if they should come to Wyomink in the spring? The governor gave him for answer that they should not suffer them to settle, and expected to be informed of everything that they should attempt, either at Wyomink or in any other part of the country. To which Teedyuscung replied that he looked upon himself as the governor's eye and ear, and that he would give him the earliest intelligence of everything that should come to his knowledge. Then Teedyuscung desired that, as the people who came with him were poor and naked, the governor would order them clothes and provisions for their journey home, and the governor promised to consult with the provincial commissioners and give him an answer. Another council was held April 13, at which was present Lieutenant Governor Hamilton and others. The governor, upon reconsidering that part of his speech to Teedyuscung, in which he desired him not to suffer the Connecticut people to settle at Wyomink, was of opinion that they might possibly misunderstand his meaning and look upon it as an encouragement for them to use force in the preventing of their settlement, by which means many murders might happen and an Indian war be revived, thought proper to explain himself more particularly on that head, for which purpose he sent for Teedyuscung and explained himself in the following manner: "Brother, by what I said to you the other day about your not suffering the Connecticut people to settle themselves at Wyomink or on any of the Indian lands, I did not mean that you should use force or proceed to kill any of them for coming amongst you and attempting to settle your lands, but you should rather collect the ancient and discreet men of your nation and go to them in a peaceable manner and endeavor to persuade them to forbear settling those lands till the right to the same should be settled by lawful authority, and the Indians to whom the land of right belongs shall consent to sell it." Teedyuscung being asked if he understood what was said, answered that he perfectly well understood it and was pleased with it. As for him he will do nothing more in this matter, but will acquaint the governor with anything that shall hereafter be attempted by these people, and leave it to the governor to do what is proper. He then acquainted the governor by a string of wampum that some of the Opey and Mohican nations were going to settle at Wyomink, and when he looked that way he should see them sitting together as one people. He will always do from his heart what shall be for the best, and in an open way. The governor then enforced again to him not to have recourse to violence lest it should occasion fresh disturbances, but that since he has said he would refer the matter to him, he will take care to manage the matter so as may be most for the interest of the Indians. In the case of Van Horn vs. Dorrance and Fenn vs. Pickering, the deposition of Parshall Terry was read. It contains *inter alia* this information: "That in the year 1762, he then being an inhabitant of Goshen, in the then province of New York, and he then also being a proprietor in the Connecticut-Susquehanna purchase, being informed that the company of proprietors had granted two townships, ten miles square each, as a gratuity to the first two hundred settlers, they being proprietors (or in proportion to a less number), conditional, that said settlers go and remain in possession for the company for the term of five years; that as near as he can recollect, some time about the last of August of the same year the deponent, with ninety-three others, mostly from Connecticut, went to Wyoming; that they carried on and took with them horses and farming utensils for the purpose of carrying on the farming business * * * The deponent saith that on their arrival at Wyoming they encamped at the mouth of Mill Creek, on the banks of the Susquehanna, where they built several huts for shelter; that they cut grass and made hay on Jacob's Plains; that they were shortly after joined by many others; that their whole company on the ground were one hundred and fifty or upwards; that they continued on the ground, according to his best recollection, about ten days; that the season being far advanced and finding that it would be difficult to procure provisions at so great distance from any inhabited country, the committee of the settlers, viz., John Jenkins, John Smith and Stephen Gardner, thought proper and advised us to return, which was agreed to and the greatest part of the company withdrew, the deponent being one;

that a small number were left on the ground who tarried some time longer as the deponent understood. The deponent says that at the time they arrived at Wyoming there were no inhabitants in that country to his knowledge, except one Teedyuscung, an Indian chief, and a number of Indian families. The deponent did not discover any appearance of any improvements being made by white people previous to the deponent and the company aforesaid going on to the lands. The deponent further saith that at the time they withdrew they secured their farming utensils in the ground to be ready for the spring following, as they expected to return at that time." A private conference was held at the governor's house in Philadelphia, November 19, 1762, Lieutenant Governor Hamilton being present. The governor desired Teedyuscung to speak nothing but what should be strictly true, which he promised to do, and then he began his business, saying: "Brother, you may remember that some time ago I told you that I should be obliged to remove from Wyomink on account of the New England people, and I now again acquaint you that soon after I returned to Wyomink from Lancaster" (August) "there came one hundred and fifty of those people, furnished with all sorts of tools, as well for building as husbandry, and declared that they bought those lands from the Six Nations and would settle them, and were actually going to build themselves houses and settle upon a creek called Lechawanoch, about seven or eight miles above Wyomink. I threatened them hard and declared I would carry them to the governor at Philadelphia, and when they heard me threaten them in this manner they said they would go away and consult their own governor, for if they were carried to Philadelphia they might be detained there seven years, and they said further, that since the Indians were uneasy at this purchase, if they would give them back the money it had cost them, which was one or two bushels of dollars, they would give them their land again. Brother, ten days after these were gone there came other fourteen men and made us the same speeches, declaring that they expected above three thousand would come and settle the Wyomink lands in the spring, and they had with them a saw and saw mill tools, purposing to go directly and build a saw mill about a mile above where I live, but upon my threatening those in the same manner I did the former company they went away, and as I was told, buried their tools somewhere in the woods. These people desired me to assist them in surveying the lands, and told me they would reward me handsomely for my trouble, but I refused to have anything to do with them. Brother, six days after these were gone there came other eight white men and a mulatto, and said the very same things to me that the others had said, and immediately I got together my counsel and as soon as we had finished our consultations I told these people that I would actually confine them and carry them to Philadelphia and deliver them to the governor there, upon which they went away saying they would go to their own governor and come again with greater numbers in the spring. Some of these people stole my horse that I bought at Easton, but they gave me another horse and five pounds in money in satisfaction for my horse. Brother, tho' I threatened these people hard that I would confine them and carry them down to you, yet I did not mean actually to do it, remembering that you charged me not to strike any white men tho' they should come, but to send you the earliest notice of their coming that was in my power. Brother, before I got up to Wyomink from Lancaster, there had come a great body of these New England people with intent actually to settle the land, but the Six Nations passing by at that time from Lancaster, sent to let them know that they should not be permitted to settle any of these lands, and on their expressing great resentment against them and threatening them if they persisted, they went away. This I was told by Thomas King, who was left behind at Wyomink by the Six Nations to tell me that they intended to lay this whole matter before the great council at Onondago, and that they would send for me and my Indians to come to Albany in the spring, where they are to have a meeting with the New England people, and desired I would be quiet till I should receive their message, and then come to Albany. On this speech of Thomas King's we met together in council and agreed not to give him any promise to come to Albany, but to advise the governor of Pennsylvania of this and to take his advice what to do, and if he will go with us and advise us to go, we will go in case we should be sent for in the spring. Brother, surely, as you have a general of the king's armies here he might hinder these people from coming and disturbing us in our possessions. * * * Brother, I have one thing more to say, and then I shall have finished all I have to say at this time. Brother, you may remember that at the treaty at Easton we were promised that a school master and ministers should be sent to instruct us in religion and to teach us to read and write. As none have been yet provided for us I desire to know what you intend to do in this matter. I have now done." The governor answered Teedyuscung's speech the next day as follows: "I thank you for the information you have given me of what passed between you and the people of Connecticut. Hearing that some of these people were gone towards the Susquehanna, I sent a special messenger after them to warn them from settling those lands and to take care not to give offense to the Indians from whom those lands had not been purchased. My messenger came, fortunately, just after the Six Nations had ordered them to go away and shown great reluctance at their presuming to come and settle those lands, and met them returning home displeased with the Six Nations for speaking to them in the rough manner they did. Brother, I have written both to General Amherst and to Sir William Johnson and to the governor of Connecticut; this matter is likewise laid before the great king by Sir William Johnson, so that I am in hopes you will not see any more of these troublesome people, but that measures will be taken to keep them at home. Brother, I commend you for your prudent behavior; I did and do still desire that no blood of the white people may be shed by you, but that you will continue to give me the earliest notice you can if you hear of any of them coming again in the spring. Brother, * * * you know that your uncles, the Six Nations, have kindled a fire for you at Wyomink, and desired you would stay there and watch and give them notice if any white people should come to take away their lands from them and that you would not suffer them to do it. You may think, be assured, that this winter measures will be taken to prevent these troublesome people from coming to disturb you. On these considerations I desire you will remain quiet where you are and not move away, as you seem to have no inclinations to go away, only on account of these New England disturbers. As to any invitations the Six Nations may make to you to come to Albany to council with them and to meet the New England people, you will pay such regard to them as your connections with your uncles will require. I don't pretend to any authority over you, but I would advise you to comply with such invitation as you shall receive from your uncles. I am not invited and know nothing of this matter, but if I hear anything of it I will let you know. The times have been so unsettled that there has been no opportunity of sending ministers and school masters among you. Now there is a likelihood of a general peace here soon established; if you determine still to continue at Wyomink, about which you have expressed some doubts to me, I shall consider of this matter and send you an answer at the proper time."

This was the last official act of Teedyuscung with the government of Pennsylvania.

For a period of nearly five years succeeding the last treaty held at Easton, the frontiers of Pennsylvania were exempt from Indian hostilities or depredations, except the practice of horse stealing, to which the savages were always addicted. The Indians frequently visited Philadelphia in parties and received attention and presents from the governor. In 1762 the chain of friendship between them and the whites was strengthened and brightened at a great council held at Lancaster, attended by chiefs from the Six Nations, by the western Indians and by those in Pennsylvania. At this treaty Teedyuscung withdrew the imputation of forgery made at Easton against the younger Penn's and their agents, but adhered to the charge of fraud as connected with the walking purchase. He, however, signed a release for all claims upon lands on the Delaware, and received for himself and his people seven hundred pounds, Pennsylvania currency (eighteen hundred dollars), in money and goods. The Moravians reëstablished their missions at Gnadenhutten, Waughwawame (Wyoming), Wyalusing and at other points, and the whites on the frontiers, recovering from the effects of the last long and bloody war were anticipating the blessings of a prosperous peace. Though suffering many privations, the zeal of the missionaries did not cool, neither did their faith waver, nor their efforts relax; their souls seemed to glow with a divine ardor, success crowned their labors, and several hundred Indians received the rite of baptism. In the meantime Wyoming was the theatre of highly interesting events. The correspondence between the executive of Pennsylvania and Sir William Johnson was reopened and the influence of the baronet was exerted upon the Six Nations to persuade them to disavow the sale of 1754. Those of the Indians who had not been concerned in the sale, and who, on the other hand, were doubtless opposed to it, were of course not unwilling to repudiate the transaction, and a deputation of five of their chiefs was sent to Hartford, accompanied by Colonel Guy Johnson, deputy agent, and an interpreter sent by Sir William. Conferences were held by these chiefs with the governor of Connecticut and his council on May 28 and 30, 1762, in the course of which the sale of the land was disavowed as a national transaction. They admitted that a sale had been made, but denied its validity, inasmuch, they averred, as it had not been made according to ancient usage in a full and open council, but the chiefs who had signed the deed had been applied to separately, and had acted only in their individual capacities. Governor Fitch, in reply, assured the chiefs that the movements of the company had not been authorized by the government, and with their proceedings it had, in fact, had nothing to do. For their further satisfaction, moreover, the governor informed them that orders had been received from his majesty commanding him to use his authority and influence to prevent the intended movement upon the lands in dispute until the matter should be laid before the king. They were likewise still farther assured that the company had acquiesced in those orders and had unanimously agreed that no person should enter upon the lands until his majesty's pleasure should be known. With these assurances, the deputies, consisting of one Mohawk, two Onondagoes and two Cayugas—none of them chiefs of note—seem to have been satisfied. But whatever might have been the desire of the shareholders of the company, the individuals who had resolved to emigrate gave little attention to their stipulations with the governor, and their advance was met by a series of unheeded proclamations and followed by the powerless remonstrances of the sheriff and magistracy residing in Northampton county, on the Delaware, to which the valley of Wyoming was held to belong, the seat of justice of which was at Easton. Nor was this all. In the course of the same year the proprietaries of Pennsylvania made a case and took the opinion of the attorney general of the crown (Mr. Pratt, afterwards Lord Camden), as to the right of Connecticut to the territory she was claiming. That officer was clear in his opinion against Connecticut—holding that, by virtue of her adjustment of boundaries with New York, she was precluded from advancing a step beyond. But the Susquehanna company was not idle. Colonel Eliphalet Dyer, a leading associate and a man of energy and ability, was dispatched to England, charged likewise with a "case," carefully prepared, which was presented to the consideration of eminent counsel in London, who came to a directly opposite conclusion. Each party therefore felt strengthened by those conflicting legal opinions, and both became the more resolute in the prosecution of their claims. Meantime fresh scenes were opening in the disputed territory, as painful as unexpected. Notwithstanding a proclamation issued by Governor Fitch, eight days after the conference with the Indians were ended, forbidding the people of Connecticut from trespassing upon the disputed territory, the pioneers who, in the summer of 1762, had commenced their operations in Wyoming, returned to the valley to resume their labors early in the ensuing spring, accompanied by their families, and with augmented numbers of settlers. They were furnished with an adequate supply of provisions, and took with them a quantity of live stock, cattle, horses and pigs. Thus provided, and calculating to draw largely from the teeming soil in the course of the season, they resumed their labors with light hearts and vigorous arms. The forests rapidly retreated before their well directed blows, and in the course of the summer they commenced bringing the lands into cultivation on both sides of the river. Their advancement was now so rapid that it is believed the jealousies of the Indians began to be awakened. At least, notwithstanding the claims which the Six Nations had asserted over the territory by virtue of which they had sold to the Susquehanna company, Teedyuscung and his people alleged that they ought to receive compensation also. Sir William Johnson had indeed predicted as much in a letter addressed to Governor Fitch in the preceding month of November, in which he said: "I cannot avoid giving you my sentiments as I formerly did, that the Indians insist upon the claims of the people of Connecticut to lands on the Susquehanna as unlawful, and the steps taken to obtain the same to be unjust, and have declared themselves determined to oppose any such settlement. I am therefore apprehensive of any farther attempt at an establishment there will not only be severely felt by those who shall put the same in execution, but may (notwithstanding all my endeavors to the contrary) be productive of fatal consequences on our frontiers." Thus matters stood until in the spring, when an event occurred which broke up the settlement at one fell blow. Indian revenge may sleep, but never dies; the hour may be postponed for months or years, but at last will come as sure as fate. Teedyuscung had slain with his own hand the chief who commanded the Iroquois war party in their devastation of Gnadenhutten. War upon the whites being now renewed, it is not improbable that the king may have declined to lead his tribe to battle. At the great council held at Easton in 1758, the Six Nations had observed, with no very cordial feelings, the important position which Teedyuscung had attained in the opinion of the whites, by the force of his talents and the energy of his character. Long accustomed to view the Delawares and their derivative tribes as their *subjects*, the haughty Iroquois could not brook this advancement of a supposed inferior, and the reflection had been rankling in their bosoms until it was determined to cut off the object of their hate. Certain, however, it is, that for some time several of the Six Nations had been visiting at Wyoming without any ostensible object, mingling, socially, with the Delawares, and appearing on friendly terms with the old chief. Whiskey had been obtained, which, when in his power, the Indian propensity was too strong to be resisted, and he drank until inebriation overpowered his senses, and he lay sleeping in his wigwam scarcely conscious of life, and wholly unsuspicious of danger. In the dead of night, on April 19, 1763, the house of Teedyuscung, and twenty of the surrounding dwellings burst, almost at the same moment, into flames, and thus the great Delaware king miserably perished. The wickedness of this deed of darkness was heightened by an act of still greater atrocity. They charged the assassination upon the white settlers from Connecticut, and had the address to inspire the Delawares with such a belief. The consequences may readily be anticipated. Teedyuscung was greatly beloved by his people, and their exasperation at "the deep damnation of his taking off," was kindled to a degree of corresponding intensity. The white settlers, however, being entirely innocent of the transaction—utterly unconscious that it had been imputed to them—were equally unconscious of the storm that was so suddenly to break upon their heads. Their intercourse with the Indians, during the preceding year, had been so entirely friendly that they had not even provided themselves with weapons of self defense, and although there had been some slight manifestations of jealousy at their onward progress, among the Indians, yet their pacific relations, thus far, had not been interrupted. But they were now reposing in false security. Stimulated to revenge by the representations of their false and insidious visitors, the Delawares, on the 15th of October, rose upon the settlement and massacred twelve of the people in cold blood, at noonday, while engaged in the labors of the field on the flats in the lower part of this city. Those who escaped ran to the adjacent plantations to apprize them of what had happened, and were the swift messengers of the painful intelligence to the houses of the settlement and the families of the slain. It was an hour of sad consternation. Having no arms even for self defense, the people were compelled at once to seize upon such few of their effects as they could carry upon their shoulders, and flee to the mountains. As they turned back, during their ascent, to steal an occasional glance at the beautiful valley below, they beheld the savages driving their cattle away to their own towns, and plundering their houses of the goods that had been left. At nightfall the torch was applied and the darkness that hung over the vale was illuminated by the lurid flames of their own dwellings—the abodes of happiness and peace in the morning. Hapless, indeed, was the condition of the fugitives. Their number amounted to several hundreds—men, women and children—the infant at the breast, the happy wife a few brief hours before, now a widow in the midst of a group of orphans. The supplies, both of provisions and clothing, which they had secured in the moment of their flight, were altogether inadequate to their wants. The chilly winds of autumn were howling with melancholy wail among the mountain pines, through which, over rivers and glens, and fearful morasses, they were to thread their way sixty miles to the nearest settlements on the Delaware and thence back to their friends in Connecticut, a distance of two hundred and fifty miles. Notwithstanding the hardships they were compelled to encounter, and the deprivations under which they labored, many of them accomplished the journey in safety, while others, lost in the mazes of the swamps, were never heard of more.

Parshall Terry says: "That early in the month of May (as near as he can recollect), in the year 1763, he, the deponent, with a small number of others, went on to Wyoming to renew their possessions; that they were soon joined by a large number, being mostly those who had been on the preceding year; that they took on with them horses, oxen, cows and farming utensils; that they proceeded to plowing, planting corn and sowing grain of different kinds, building houses, fences and all kinds of farmers business; that they made large improvements in Wilkes-Barre, Kingston, Plymouth and Hanover (as they are now called); that they improved several hundred acres of land with corn and other grain, and procured a large quantity of hay; that they carried on their business unmolested until the month of October; that during their residence at Wyoming this season, according to his best recollection, there were about one hundred and fifty settlers who made improvements, though not so great a number on the ground at any one time; that he also well recollects lands being laid out and lotted on the Susquehanna river the same year, and that he, the deponent, drew a lot at that time in Wilkes-Barre (as it is now called); that on the fifteenth day of October the settlers being in a scattered condition, on their respective farms, they were attacked by the savages, surprised in every part of their settlement, and all at or near the same time; that near twenty were killed of the settlers, the others taken and dispersed. The whole of the property of the settlers then on the ground fell into the enemy's hands. The deponent recollects the names of several that were killed, viz., the Rev. William Marsh, Thomas Marsh, Timothy Hollister, Timothy Hollister, junior, Nathaniel Hollister, Samuel Richards, Nathaniel Terry, Wright Smith, Daniel Baldwin and his wife, Jesse Wiggins, and a woman by the name of Zeriah Whitney. Several others were killed whose names he does not recollect." In an appendix to an address delivered at the Wyoming Monument by W. H. Egle, M. D., July 3, 1889, we have a brief narrative of the captivity of Isaac Hollister. He says: "On the 15th day of October, 1763, as I was at work with my father on the banks of the Susquehannah, the Indians to the number of one hundred and thirty-five came upon us, and killed my father on the spot. My brother, Timothy, who was at work about half mile distant under-went the same fate, as did likewise fourteen or fifteen others who were at work in different places. The Indians, after they had burnt and destroyed all they could, marched off, and carried me up the Susquehannah river about one hundred and fifty miles."

The names of the survivors were John Jenkins, William Bâck, Oliver Smith, Abel Pierce, Obadiah Gore, Daniel Gore, Isaac Underwood, Isaac Bennett, James Atherton, Ebenezer Searles, Ephraim Taylor, Ephraim Taylor, Jr., John Dorrance, Timothy Smith, Jonathan Slocum, Benjamin Follett, Nathan Hurlbut, Isaac Hollister, Matthew Smith, Benjamin Davis, George Minor, John Smith, Eliphalet Stevens, William Stevens, Ephraim Seely, David Honeywell, Jonathan Weeks, Jonathan Weeks, Jr., Philip Weeks, Uriah Stevens, Gideon Lawrence, Stephen Gardner, Augustus Hunt, John Comstock, Oliver Jewell, Ezra Dean, Daniel Larence, Ezekiel Pierce, Elkanah Fuller, Benjamin Ashley, Stephen Lee, ——— Hover, Silas Parke, Moses Kimball, Nathaniel Chapman, Benjamin Shoemaker, Simeon Draper, David Marvin, Parshall Terry.

The descendants of a large number of the above named persons still reside in the Wyoming valley, having returned in 1769, when the next attempt at settlement was made.

Teedyuscung with all his faults, was yet one of the noblest of his race. Yet, his character stands not well in history—not as well, by any means, as it deserves. That he was a man of talent and courage, there can be no question ; but withal he was greatly subject to the constitutional infirmities of his race, unstable in his purposes, and a lover of the fire waters—the enemy which, received to the lip, steals away the brain, alike of the white man and the red. It has already been seen that he was early a convert—and apparently a sincere one—to the christian faith of the missionaries. After the suspension of hostilities, and during negotiations for peace, he was much at Bethlehem, and at one time fixed his residence there. His attachment to the brethren he openly avowed, expressing his determination to keep by them in preference to others of the whites. Elsewhere he exulted in being called a Moravian. Although he had broken his vows and had been unfaithful to his profession, he would frequently, when in conversation with the brethren, revert to his baptism, and feelingly deplore the loss of the peace of mind he had once enjoyed. And hence we doubt not that there were times when, marshalling his savage warriors for deeds of blood in the wild highlands of the Delawares, there would come over him a vision of the "Huts of Grace," in the peaceful valley of the Mahoning, and of the turreted chapel in which he had knelt in baptism, and which he had entered so often on holy days, at the sound of the church-going bell. But his faith was too weak to withstand the influence of ambition, and when elevated to the supreme chieftainship of the scattering tribes of his nation, his behavior was such as to cause the good missionaries to tremble for his safety, seeing that he became "like a reed shaken by the wind." Hitherto, for many years, his nation had been down-trodden by the Iroquois, but when they determined once more to assert their own manhood, and to grasp the hatchet presented them by the French, electing Teedyuscung their king, as he had been their energetic champion in the councils before, he now became, as he was called, "The Trumpet of War." He did not, however, long continue upon the war path, but, as has been seen, became an early advocate and ambassador of peace, although his sincerity in this respect was questioned by the Moravian clergy and likewise by Sir William Johnson. Still it must be recorded in his behalf that he appears never to have entirely forfeited the confidence of the Quakers. They were indeed opposed to the declaration of war against the Indians by Governor Hamilton—believing that the difficulties with them might have been healed by a more pacific course. And in this view they had the concurrence of Sir William Johnson. But in regard to the character of Teedyuscung, the sympathies of the baronet were with his own Indians—the Six Nations. They hated, and finally murdered him, and Sir William loved him not. Yet in his correspondence, while he labored to detract somewhat from the lofty pretensions of the Delaware captain, the baronet has conceded to him enough of talent, influence and power among his people to give him a proud rank among the chieftains of his race. Certain it is, that Teedyuscung did much to restore his nation to the rank of Men, of which they had been deprived by the Iroquois, and great allowances are to be made on the score of his instability of conduct, from the peculiar circumstances under which he was often placed. In regard to his religious character and professions, his memory rests beneath a cloud. There were seasons, according to the records of the faithful missionary, in which he gave signs of penitence and reform. The brethren did all in their power for his reclamation. Occasional appearances of contrition at times inspired hopes of success. "As to externals," he once said, "I possess everything in plenty; but riches are of no use to me, for I have a troubled conscience. I still remember well what it is to feel peace in the heart, but now I have lost all." Yet he soon turned back. All hopes of his case were lost, and in recording his death, the benevolent Loskiel briefly says: "He was burnt in his house at Wajomick, without having given any proof of repentance."

The following authorities in part have been consulted in compiling this paper:

Chapman, I. A. History of Wyoming.
Colonial Records.
Day, Sherman. Historical Collections of the State of Pennsylvania.
Egle, W. H., M. D. History of Pennsylvania.
Hollister, H., M. D. History of the Lackawanna Valley.
Hoyt, H. M. Brief of a Title in the Seventeen Townships.
Miner, Charles. History of Wyoming.
Montgomery, Morton L. Indians of Pennsylvania in Dr. Egle's Historical Register.
Pearce, Stewart. Annals of Luzerne County.
Pennsylvania Archives.
Reichel, W. C. Memorials of the Moravian Church.
Stone, W. L. Poetry and History of Wyoming.

COAL:

ITS ANTIQUITY.

DISCOVERY AND EARLY DEVELOPMENT IN THE WYOMING VALLEY.

COAL, ITS ANTIQUITY. DISCOVERY AND EARLY DEVELOPMENT IN THE WYOMING VALLEY.

[Paper read before the Wyoming Historical and Geological Society, June 27, 1890, by George B. Kulp, Esq., Historiographer of the Society.]

The word Coal has been derived by some writers from the Hebrew, and by others from the Greek or Latin, but whatever may be its origin, it is deserving of remark that the same sound for the same object is used in the Anglo-Saxon, the Teutonic, the Dutch, the Danish and the Islandic languages.

In its most general sense the term Coal includes all varieties of carbonaceous minerals used as fuel. Stone coal is a local English term, but with a signification restricted to the substance known by mineralogists as anthracite. In old English writings the terms pit coal and sea coal are commonly used. These have reference to the mode in which the mineral is obtained and the manner in which it is transported to market. Anthracite is the most condensed form of mineral coal and the richest in carbon. Its color varies from jet to glistening black, to dark lead gray; it is clean, not soiling the hands; ignites with difficulty; burns with a short blue flame without smoke, and with very little illuminating power. It gives an intense, concentrated heat. Some varieties when undisturbed while burning, partially retain their shape till nearly consumed, and some become extinct before they have parted with the whole of their carbon. The constituents of anthracite are carbon, water and earthy matters—not in chemical proportions, but in accidental and varying mixtures. There are also other ingredients occasionally present, beside the oxide of iron, silica and alumina, which compose the earthy matters or ash. These are sulphur, bitumen, &c. All coals, including in this designation naphtha, petroleum, asphaltum, &c., are but representatives of the successive changes from vegetable to mineral matters. Anthracite is the condensed coke of bituminous coal. It must be borne in mind that the signification now attached to the word coal is different from that which formerly obtained, when wood was the only fuel in general use. Coal then meant the carbonaceous residue obtained in the destructive distillation of wood, or what is known as charcoal, and the name collier was applied indifferently to both coal miners and charcoal burners. The spelling "cole" was generally used up to the middle of the seventeenth century when it was gradually superseded by the modern form "coal." The plural coals seems to have been used from a very early period to signify the broken fragments of the mineral as prepared for use.

The use of mineral coal as fuel certainly antedates the Christian era, but the date of the earliest mining operations is unknown. A paragraph from the writings of Theophrastus, one of Aristotle's disciples, who was born in the year 382 B. C., is quoted to prove its early use, but as no reference is made to mining operations, it seems probable that the coal gathered and "broken for use" was loose outcrop coal. The passage reads: "Those substances that are called coals and are broken for use are earthy, but they kindle and burn like wooden coals. They are found in Lyguria, where there is amber, and in Ellis, over the mountain towards Olympias. They are used by the smiths." The word "coal" frequently occurring in the Bible, is doubtless used to denote wood, charcoal, or any substance used as fuel. The ancient Britons had a primitive name for this fossil, and Pennant says: "That a flint axe, the instrument of the Aborigines of our island, was discovered in a certain vein of coal in Monmouthshire, and in such a situation as to render it very accessible to the inexperienced natives who, in early times, were incapable of pursuing the seams to any great depths." Cæsar takes no notice of coal in his description of England, yet there is good evidence to believe that the Romans brought it into use. In the West Riding of Yorkshire are many beds of cinders, heaped up in the fields, in one of which a number of Roman coins were found some years ago. From Horsely it appears that there was a colliery at Benwell, about four miles west of New Castle upon Tyne, supposed to have been actually worked by the Romans, and it is evident from Whitaker that coals were used as fuel in England by the Saxons. No mention is made of this fossil during the Danish occupation, nor for many years after the Norman conquest. The first charter for the license of digging coals was granted by King Henry III in the year 1239; it was there denominated sea coal, and in 1281 Newcastle was famous for its great trade in this article. The privilege of digging coal in the lands of Pittencrief, was conferred by charter on the abbot and convent of Dumferline in 1291, and at a very early period the monks of Newbattle Abbey dug coal from surface-pits on the banks of the Esk. In 1306 the use of sea coal was prohibited in London from its supposed tendency to corrupt the air. Shortly after this it was the common fuel at the King's palace in London, and in 1325 a trade was opened between France and England in which corn was imported and coal was exported. Aeneas Silvius Piccolomini (afterwards Pope Pius II), who visited Scotland in the fifteenth century, refers to the fact that the poor people received at the church doors a species of stone which they burned in place of wood, but, although the value of coal for smiths and artificers' work was early recognized, it was not generally employed for domestic purposes till about the close of the sixteenth century. In 1606 an Act was passed binding colliers to perpetual service at the works at which they were engaged, and their full emancipation did not take place until 1799.

In 1615 there were employed in the coal trade of New Castle four hundred sail of ships, one-half of which supplied

London, the remainder the other part of the kingdom. The French, too, are represented as trading to New Castle at this time for coal, in fleets of fifty sails at once, serving the ports of Picardy, Normandy, Rochelle and Bordeaux, while the ships of Bremen, Emboden, Holland and Zealand were supplying the inhabitants of Flanders.

Macaulay, in his History of England, says that "coal, though very little used in any species of manufacture, was already the ordinary fuel in some districts which were fortunate enough to possess large beds, and in the capital, which could easily be supplied by water carriage. It seems reasonable to believe that at least one-half of the quantity then extracted from the pits was consumed in London. The consumption of London seemed to the writers of that age enormous, and was often mentioned by them as a proof of the greatness of the imperial city. They scarcely hoped to be believed when they affirmed that two hundred and eighty thousand chaldrons, that is to say, about three hundred and fifty thousand tons, were, in the last year of the reign of Charles the Second (1685), brought to the Thames."

Coal mining was also prosecuted in Scotland in the eleventh and in Germany in the thirteenth century, while at the antipodes the Chinese had even at that early day become familiar with the use of coal.

Saward, in his Coal Trade for 1890, speaks thus of the coal supplies of the world:

"In view of the question which has suggested itself on more than one occasion as to how long it would be before the Old World coal deposits would become exhausted, a German scientific journal supplies some interesting figures relating to the world's coal fields outside of the North American Continent. According to these, the Low Countries, Switzerland, Denmark, Germany, and Bohemia possess coal mines of a surface area of about fifty-nine thousand square miles. Russia alone has twenty-two thousand square miles.

The deposits of the island of Formosa amount to something like ten thousand square miles, some of the coal veins ranging up to 96 feet in thickness. The coal fields of Austria, Spain, Portugal, Italy, Greece, Turkey, and Persia cover about thirty-nine thousand square miles, those of India thirty-five thousand, and those of Japan six thousand square miles, while those of China are estimated at the enormous figure of four hundred thousand square miles. But these are not all. The Falkland Islands, Patagonia, and Peru are very rich in coal, while the southern part of Chili is one immense deposit. In Brazil veins varying in thickness from seventeen to twenty-five feet are found in numbers, and in the United States of Columbia there is an abundance of the mineral. Mexico and the Vancouver Islands are also well supplied, there being probably not far from twenty thousand square miles, while the deposits thus far discovered in Tasmania, New Caledonia, and Natal are estimated to cover one hundred thousand square miles; the larger number of these deposits have not yet been worked."

But it was not until the eighteenth century that coal mining began to be scientifically prosecuted. Prior to that time the mines were of very limited depth, rarely going beneath water level; the coal was raised by a windlass or horse-gin, drainage affected by adits, or the water was raised in chain pumps or barrels operated by hand or horse-power, and the natural ventilation—aided in some instances by falling water, and later by furnaces—was usually the sole reliance for removing foul air and explosive gases.

Yet in some of these early operations there are pictures not unlike those to be seen every day at our modern mines; thus the following description of the early tram-roads and wagons used at Newcastle, from "The History and Antiquities of the Town of New Castle, upon Tyne," by John Brand, M. A., 1789, in which an article written by Lord

Keeper Guilder, 1676, quoted below, singularly resembles the present practice:

"The manner of carriage is by laying rails of timber from the colliery down to the river, exactly straight and parallel; and bulky carts are made with four rowlets, fitting these rails, whereby the carriage is so easy that one horse will draw four or five chaldrons of coals, and is an immense benefit to the coal merchants."

The fate of many who embarked in mining at that time is strikingly similar to that which frequently overtakes the projectors of enterprises at present, as evinced by the following from Grey's "Chorographia," 1649:

"One merchant imployeth five hundred or a thousand in his works of coal; yet, for all of his labour, care and cost, can scarcely live by his trade; nay, many of them hath consumed and spent great estates and dyed beggars. I can remember one, of many, that raysed his estate by coale trade; many I remember that hath wasted great estates."

"Some South gentlemen have, upon great hope of benefit, come into this country to hazard their monies in coale pits. Master Beaumont, a gentleman of great inginuity and rare parts, adventured into our mines with his thirty thousand pounds; who brought with him many rare engines, not known then in these parts—as, the art to boore with iron rodds, to try the deepnesse and thicknesse of the coale, rare engines to draw water out of the pits, wagons with one horse, to carry down coales from the pits to the stathes to the river. * * * In a few years he consumed all his money, and rode home upon his light-horse."

As it is with anthracite we have to deal, we will devote ourselves to that branch of coal. Of the value or even the existence of coal in America all races were ignorant until the eighteenth century. "At Christian Spring, near Nazareth, Pa., there was living about the year 1750 to 1755, a gunsmith, who, upon application being made him by several

Indians to repair their rifles, replied that he was unable to comply immediately; 'for,' said he, 'I am entirely bare of charcoal, but as I am now engaged in setting some wood to char it, therefore, you must wait several weeks.' This, the Indians, having come a great distance, felt loath to do; they demanded a bag from the gunsmith, and having received it, went away and in two hours returned with as much stone coal as they could well carry. They refused to tell where they had procured it." As there is no coal near Nazareth the tale seems improbable. If the time fixed had been two days, instead of two hours, the coal could have been brought from the Mauch Chunk region in that time. That portion of Pennsylvania purchased of the Five Nations by the Connecticut-Susquehanna Company at Albany, N. Y., July 11, 1754, for the sum of two thousand pounds of current money of the province of New York, embraced the Lackawanna and Wyoming coal district. Fourteen years later, November 5, 1768, the same territory was included in the Fort Stanwix purchase of the Indian Nations by the proprietary government of Pennsylvania. The strife between Pennsylvania and Connecticut resulted from these purchases. The first notice of coal at Wyoming grew out of the settlement there in 1762. Parshall Terry, in his deposition, says:

"As near as he can recollect, some time about the last of August, 1762, he, with ninety-three others, mostly from Connecticut, went to Wyoming, encamped at the mouth of Mill Creek, on the bank of the Susquehanna, built huts, made hay on Jacob's Plains, and shortly after were joined by many others, and they continued there ten days or longer. The committee of the settlers, viz.: John Jenkins, John Smith and Stephen Gardner advised us to return, which was agreed to." After the return home of these settlers the above committee, through their chairman, John Jenkins, made report of the discovery of iron ore and anthracite coal at Wyoming.

"At a meeting of the Susquehanna Company, held at Windham, in the county of Windham and colony of Connecticut, April 17, 1763, it appearing to this company that some of the proprietors of our purchase of lands at Susquehanna river, to the number of two or three hundred, desire that the lands may be laid out into several townships, as a part of their rights for the speedy settlement of said lands.

"It is therefore voted, That there shall be eight townships laid out on said river, as near as may be to the townships granted as gratuity to the first settlers, each of said eight townships to contain five miles square of land, fit for good improvement or equivalent thereunto as the land may suitably accommodate, at the discretion of a committee hereafter to be named and appointed for that purpose, *reserving* for the use of the company for their after-disposal, all beds or mines of iron ore and coal that may be within the towns ordered for settlement."

"This would appear to be the first discovery and mention of anthracite coal in the country."—*Dr. Egle's History of Pennsylvania.*

The next mention of coal is in a letter written by James Tilghman of Philadelphia, August 14, 1766, addressed to the Proprietaries, Thomas and Richard Penn, Spring Garden, London. At the close of four compact pages on other matters, it says: "My brother-in-law, Colonel Francis, one of the officers who lately applied to you for a grant of some lands in the Forks of the Susquehanna, when there shall be a purchase of the Indians, has lately made an excursion into those parts and has removed a good many of the people settled upon the Indian lands, partly by persuasion and partly by compulsion, which has made the Indians pretty easy, to appearance. He went up the N. E. Branch as far as Wyoming, where, he says, there is a considerable body of good lands and a very great fund of coal in the hills which surround a very fine and extensive bottom there. This coal is thought to be very fine. With his compliments he sends you a piece of this coal. This bed of coal, situate as it is on the side of the river, may some time or other be a thing of great value." By way of postscript he adds: "the coal is in a small package of the Governor's." In a reply from Thomas Penn, dated London, November 7, 1766, to Mr. Tilghman, he say in acknowledgment: "I desire you will return my thanks to Colonel Francis for his good services in removing the intruders that were settled on the Indians' land, and for the piece of coal which we shall have examined by some persons skillful in that article, and send their observations on it."

The next mention we have of coal is on the original draft of the Manor of Sunbury, surveyed in 1768 by Charles Stewart in the Proprietary's interest, where appears the brief notation "stone coal" without further explanation. The location on the draft is near the mouth of Toby's creek, and not far from where the Woodward breaker is located.

The next mention of coal is as follows: During General Sullivan's march through Wyoming, in 1779, Major George Grant, one of his officers, wrote of the valley: "The land here is excellent, and comprehends vast mines of coal, pewter, lead and copperas." The last three named have never been found here.

The next mention of coal is as follows: John David Schopf, in his *Travels*, mentions a visit he made in 1783 to a bed of brilliant black coal, a mile above Wyoming, which, on handling, leaves no taint, and burns without emitting an offensive odor; that it was so abundant as to be obtained without any charge. He further tells us that a smith had erected workshops near it, and who spoke highly of its value. He noticed the numerous impressions of plants between the shale and the coal, which he believes proves its origin and great antiquity. It is found here on both sides of the river, and in various parts of the valley.

We here conclude the notice of coal with one further mention. Joseph Scott, in his "Gazetteer of the United States," published in 1795, in his remarks on Luzerne county, says: "Wilkes-Barre, the county seat, contains forty-five dwellings, a court house and jail, and several large beds of coal are found in the townships of Wilkes-Barre, Kingston, Exeter and Plymouth.

It is impossible to state when the consumption of Wyoming coal began. It is possible that the Indians at Wyoming had some knowledge of the combustible nature of anthracite coal. Two chiefs from the valley, in company with three others from the country of the Six Nations, visited England in 1710, and it is presumed they witnessed the burning of coal, then in general use in the cities of England, for domestic purposes. The consumption of black stones instead of wood could not fail to make a deep impression on their minds, and they would naturally infer that this fuel was nearly allied to the black stones of their own country. The appearance of anthracite had long been familiar to their eyes. The forge, or seven feet vein of coal, had been cut through and exposed by the Nanticoke creek, and the seven feet vein of Plymouth had been laid open to view by Ransom's creek. The Susquehanna had exposed the coal at Pittston, and the Lackawanna at several points along its banks. If the Indians at that day were ignorant of the practical use of coal, they were at least acquainted with its appearance and not improbably with its inflamable nature. That the Indians had mines of some kind at Wyoming, the following account fully establishes:

In 1766 a company of Nanticokes and Mohicans, six in number, who had formerly lived at Wyoming, visited Philadelphia, and in their talk with the governor said: "As we came down from Chenango we stopped at Wyoming, where we had a mine in two places, and we discovered that some white people had been at work in the mine and had filled canoes with the ore, and we saw their tools with which they had dug it out of the ground, where they made a hole at least forty feet long and five or six feet deep. It happened that formerly some white people did take now and then only a small bit and carry it away, but these people have been working at the mine and filled their canoes. We inform you that there is one John Anderson, a trader, now living at Wyoming, and we suspect he or somebody by him has robbed our mine. This man has a store of goods, and it may happen that when the Indians see their mine robbed they will come and take away his goods," etc. The substance alluded to by the Indians had been carried away in small quantities for some time, by the whites, perhaps to test its qualities, and it is highly improbable that it would have been afterwards removed by canoe loads unless it had been found to be a useful article. What could that useful article have been but coal? There were settlements of whites on the Susquehanna, a little below the site of the town of Northumberland, several years before the period when these Indians had their talk with the governor, and the coal may have been taken there for blacksmithing purposes. The Indians who had their guns repaired at Christian Spring certainly had knowledge of the value of coal for combustible purposes.

Obadiah Gore, who represented Westmoreland county in the legislature of Connecticut, in 1781 and 1782, and subsequently one of the judges of Luzerne county, and in 1788, 1789 and 1790 a member of the Pennsylvania legislature, emigrated from Plainfield, Conn., to Wyoming in 1769, and began life in the new colony as a blacksmith. Friendly with the remaining natives, from motives of policy, he learned of them the whereabouts of black stones, and being withal a hearty and an experimenting artisan, he succeeded in mastering the coal to his shop purposes the same year. He, in connection with his brother, Daniel Gore, also a blacksmith, were the first white men in Wyoming to give practical recognition and development to anthracite as a generator of heat. In the few blacksmith shops in Wyoming Valley and the West Branch settlements coal was gradually introduced after its manipulation by Mr. Gore. Mr. Pearce, who differs from most of the historians of the valley, says, "We do not believe, as do some, that the Gores were the first whites who used anthracite on the Susquehanna for blacksmithing. Stone coal would not have been noted on the original draft of the Manor of Sunbury if it had not been known to be a useful article. Hence, when the first settlers came into our valley the evidence inclines us to believe the knowledge of the use of anthracite coal was communicated to them by the Indians or by some of their own race." Jesse Fell used anthracite coal in a nailery in 1788. He says, "I found it to answer well for making wrought nails, and instead of losing in the weight of the rods, the nails exceeded the weight of the rods, which was not the case when they were wrought in a charcoal furnace." When the struggle for American independence began, in 1775, the proprietary government of Pennsylvania found itself so pressed for firearms that under the sanction of the supreme executive council two Durham boats were sent up to Wyoming and loaded with coal at Mill Creek, a short distance above Wilkes-Barre, and floated down the Susquehanna to Harris Ferry (Harrisburg), thence drawn upon wagons to Carlisle, and employed in furnaces and forges to supply the defenders of our country with arms. This was done annually during the revolutionary war. Thus stone coal, by its patriotic triumphs, achieved its way into gradual use.

The Smith brothers, John and Abijah, of Plymouth, were the first in point of time who engaged in the continuing industry of the mining of anthracite coal in the United States. They left their home in Derby, Conn., in 1805–6, came to this valley and immediately purchased coal land and engaged in mining coal. There were others who had made the attempt on the Lehigh, but the obstacles and discouragements which stood in the way proved too great and the work had to be given up. It was not resumed until the year 1820. *The Smith brothers shipped their first ark of coal in the fall of 1807, to Columbia, Pa. This was probably the first cargo of anthracite coal that was ever offered for sale in this country.* In 1808 they sent several ark loads to Columbia and other points. Prior to 1803, as we believe, the use of anthracite coal as a fuel was confined almost exclusively to furnaces and forges, using an air blast, notwithstanding the fact that Oliver Evans had, in 1802, and even before that time, demonstrated on several occasions that the blast was unnecessary for the domestic use of coal, and had successfully burned the fuel in an open grate and also in a stove without an artificial draft. In order to create a market for this fuel it became necessary to show that it could be used for domestic purposes as well as in furnaces and forges; that it was a better and more convenient fuel than wood, and that its use was attended with no difficulties. To accomplish this the Smiths went with their coal arks sent to market, and took with them a stone mason and several grates, with the purpose of setting the grates in the public houses where they might make known the utility of their fuel. In several houses in Columbia and in other towns the fire places for burning wood were changed by them and fitted for the use of coal, and coal fires were lighted, careful instructions being given meanwhile in the mysteries of a stone coal fire. After much perseverance and expense in providing coal and grates to demonstrate the valuable qualities of the new fuel, they disposed of a small part of their cargo and left the rest to be sold on commission. Notwithstanding the thorough manner in which they had set about the introduction of coal as a fuel for domestic uses, it was several years before all obstacles to its use were overcome and they were able to gain a profit from the enterprise.

The annual average of the business of the Messrs. Smith from 1807 down to 1820 was from six to eight ark loads, or about four to five hundred tons. "The old Susquehanna coal ark, like the mastodon, is a thing of the past. The present men of the business should understand the character of the simple vessel used by the pioneers of the trade. Its size and dimensions, cost and capacity must be chronicled. The length of the craft was ninety feet, its width sixteen feet, its depth four feet, and its capacity 60 tons. Each end terminated in an acute angle, with a stem post surmounted by a huge oar some thirty feet in length, and which required the strength of two stout men to ply it in the water. It required in its construction thirty-eight hundred feet of two inch plank for the bottom, ends and sides, or seventy-six hundred feet board measure. The bottom timbers would contain about two thousand feet board measure, and the ribs or studs sustaining the side planks four hundred feet, making a total of some ten thousand feet. The ark was navigated by four men, and the ordinary time to reach tide water was seven days. Two out of three arks would probably reach the port of their destination; one-third was generally left upon the rocks in the rapids of the river or went to the bottom." The average price of sales at this time was probably ten dollars, leaving a profit of five dollars on the ton. If, therefore, three hundred and fifty tons of the five hundred annually transported by the Messrs. Smith reached the market, it left them a profit of seventeen hundred dollars, not taking into account their personal services. Mr. George M. Hollenback sent two ark loads down the Susquehanna, taken from his Mill Creek mines in 1813. The same year Joseph Wright of Plymouth mined two ark loads of coal from the mines of his brother, the late Samuel G. Wright, of New Jersey, near Port Griffith, in Jenkins township. This was an old

opening and coal had been mined there as far back as 1775.
The late Lord Butler of Wilkes-Barre had also shipped coal from his mines, more generally known of late years as the "Baltimore mines," as early as 1814, and so had Crandall Wilcox of Plains township. Colonel George M. Hollenback sent two four-horse loads of coal to Philadelphia in 1813, and James Lee, of Hanover, sent a four-horse load to a blacksmith in Germantown. In 1813 Hon. Charles Miner was publishing *The Gleaner* in Wilkes-Barre, and in a long editorial article from his pen, under date of November 19, and the head of "State Policy," he urged, with great zeal, the improvement of the descending navigation of the Susquehanna and Lehigh rivers. He then said: "*The coal of Wyoming has already become an article of considerable traffic with the lower counties of Pennsylvania.* Numerous beds have been opened, and it is ascertained, beyond all doubt, that the valley of Wyoming contains enough coal for ages to come." Chapman, in his History of Wyoming, writing in 1817, speaking of coal, says: "*It constitutes the principal fuel of the inhabitants as well as their most important article of exportation.*" Plumb, in his History of Hanover township, says: "*From 1810 to 1820 one thousand or fifteen hundred tons per year were mined in Hanover,*" and "*there was a constant sale of coal down the river by arks from the time people learned to burn it in the house.*" In this small way the coal trade continued on from 1807 to 1820, when it assumed more importance in the public estimation. The years preceding that of 1820 were the years of its trials, and the men, during that period, who were engaged in the business were merely able to sustain themselves with the closest economy and the most persevering and unremitting labor. The following account current rendered by Price & Waterbury, of New York, to Abijah Smith & Co., is a remarkably interesting relic of the coal business in its infancy. It very clearly exhibits two facts—one the demand, price and consumption of coal in the

great city of New York at that period, and the other, the wonderful zeal manifested in the pioneer dealers to introduce the article into the market. The coal was sent to Havre de Grace, Maryland, and thence by coasting vessels to New York:

"NEW YORK, FEBRUARY, 1813.

Messrs. Abijah Smith & Co.,

Gentlemen :—Having lately taken a view of the business we have been conducting for you this sometime past, we have thought it would be gratifying to have the account forwarded, and therefore present you with a summary of it up to the 18th of January, 1813, containing first, the quantity of coal sold, and to whom ; second, the amount of cash paid us from time to time ; third, the amount of interest cash on the various sums advanced, the credit of interest on sums received ; and lastly, the quantity of coal remaining on hand unsold. Should you on the receipt of this find any of the items incorrect, we need hardly observe that the knowledge of such an error will be corrected with the greatest pleasure. As it respects our future plan of procedure we shall expect to see one of your concern in the city sometime in the spring, when a new arrangement may be fixed upon. Our endeavors to establish the character of the coal shall not at any time be wanting, and we calculate shortly to dispose of the remaining parcels of coal unsold."

1812.	June 8.—By cash of Doty & Willets, for 5 chaldrons of coal	$ 100 00
	By cash of John Withington, for 5 chaldrons of coal	100 00
	By cash of Coulthaid & Son, for 10 chaldrons of coal	200 00
	By John Benham's note, 90 days, for 10 chaldrons of coal	200 00
	By cash of G. P. Lorrilard, for 1 chaldron of coal	20 00
	By cash of J. J. Wilson, for 4 chaldrons of coal	80 00
	June 13.—By cash of Doty & Willetts, for 5 chaldrons of coal	100 00
	By cash of G. P. Lorrilard, for 11½ chaldrons of coal	230 00
	By A. Frazyer's note, 90 days, for 25 chaldrons of coal	475 00
	By cash received of T. Coulthaid, for 5 chaldrons of coal	100 00
	By M. Womas' note, 90 days, for 20 chaldrons of coal	380 00
	By half measurement received for 9 bushels of coal	6 33
	By B. Ward and T. Blagge, for 1¼ chaldrons at $20 per chaldron	25 00
	By Wittingham, for ½ chaldron of coal	10 00
	June 25.—By Pirpont, for ½ chaldron of coal	11 00
	By Mr. Landiss, for ½ chaldron of coal	12 00
	July 16.—By Robert Barney, for 17½ chaldrons of coal at $22 per chaldron	385 00
	Sept. 15 —By cash for 1 chaldron of coal	12 50
	Oct. 9.—By William Colman, for ½ chaldron of coal	12 50
	By Sexton & Williamson, for 1½ chaldrons of coal	37 50
	Oct. 24.—By cash for 1 chaldron of coal	25 00
	Oct. 29.—By cash for ½ chaldron of coal	12 50
	Nov. 7.—By cash for ½ chaldron of coal	12 50
	Nov. 12.—By cash for 1 chaldron of coal	25 00
	Nov. 16.—By Mr. A. Le Briton, for 12 chaldrons of coal at $25 per chaldron	288 50
	Dec. 5.—By cash for ½ chaldron of coal	12 50
	Dec. 11.—By cash A. Daily, for ½ chaldron of coal	12 50
	Dec. 14.—By cash for ½ chaldron of coal	12 00
1813.	Jan. 4.—By cash for 1 chaldron of coal	25 00
	Jan. 18.—By J. Curtiz, for 9 bushels of coal	6 27
	By amount of balance this day	763 12
	Total	$3601 20

Errors excepted, Price & Waterbury.

It will be seen by this account current that coal was sold by the chaldron, thirty-six bushels, or nearly a ton and a third to the chaldron. The sales therefore, for the New York supply in 1812, by this firm, were inside of two hundred tons.

It seems to be the common belief that the anthracite coal trade had its rise on the Lehigh in the year 1820, when three hundred and sixty-five tons of coal were carried to market, yet, as a matter of fact, the industry was begun at Plymouth thirteen years before, and for nine years prior to the beginning of the coal business on the Lehigh river the annual shipments on the Susquehanna were considerably in excess of the first year's product of the Lehigh region.

Mr. Pearce states that up to 1820 "the total amount of coal sent from Wyoming is reckoned at eighty-five hundred tons." This we believe to be a low estimate. The same author states that Colonel Washington Lee, in 1820, "mined and sent to Baltimore one thousand tons, which he sold at $8 per ton." Coal had been introduced in Baltimore and sold there by the Smith Brothers prior to that date. Let us make a new *apex* to the *coal pyramids* now in use. Let it

NOTE.—The Lehigh region is great in making claims. For instance, on April 23, 1891, in the Senate of the state of Pennsylvania, Senator Rapsher of Carbon called up the following bill on third reading:

AN ACT appropriating the sum of two thousand dollars for the erection of a monument to the memory of Philip Ginter, the discoverer of anthracite coal in Pennsylvania.

SECTION 1. Be it enacted by the Senate and House of Representatives of the Commonwealth of Pennsylvania in General Assembly met, and it is hereby enacted by the authority of the same, that the sum of two thousand dollars be appropriated towards the erection of a suitable monument to commemorate the memory of Philip Ginter, the first discoverer of anthracite coal in Pennsylvania, to be paid to the committee in charge upon the warrant of the Auditor General.

Senator Hines from our own county asked leave to strike out the words "the first," because Philip Ginter was not the first discoverer of coal.

Senator Rapsher, in reply, said: Mr. President, the historians, like men, sometimes differ on that particular point, as to whether Philip Ginter was the first discoverer or not, but I think all the historians agree that Philip Ginter was the first authentic discoverer of anthracite coal in what was then Northampton county, a hundred years ago the first of next September, and it was the inception of the Lehigh Coal and Navigation Company, and was the beginning of the anthracite coal traffic in Pennsylvania, and because the anthracite coal interest was of so much importance to the State credit in our section, this could be granted without any great strain on our consciences.

Senator Green, of Berks, where they have no coal, said: Mr. President, I think we ought to have a discoverer of coal, and we might as well have him now as at any other time, so whether it is Mr. Ginter, or somebody else, makes very little difference to me. I am willing to concede to that gentleman that claim. I am willing to go further: I am willing to take the word of the senator from Carbon for it. If he thinks he is the discoverer of coal, I think so.

Fortunately the bill was defeated in the House of Representatives. Now, what was in be understood that the *commencement of the trade* was in 1807, when the Smith Brothers sent to market and sold fifty-five tons.

Commencement of the Anthracite Coal Trade in the United States:

WYOMING REGION.		LEHIGH REGION.	
1807	55 tons.		
1808	150 "		
1809	200 "		
1810	350 "		
1811	450 "		
1812	500 "		
1813	500 "		
1814	700 "		
1815	1000 "		
1816	1000 "		
1817	1100 "		
1818	1200 "		
1819	1400 "		
1820	2500 "	1820	365 tons.

The foregoing statement we believe to be absolutely correct. The pyramids now in use give the year 1829 as the commencement of the coal trade in the Lackawanna region, and seven thousand tons sent by the Delaware & Hudson Canal Company. The same pyramids start us in the Wyoming

this bill? First, to get $2000 out of the state treasury to perpetrate a *falsehood*. This under false pretences.

Second. To place on record the further *falsehood* that Philip Ginter was the (first) discoverer of anthracite coal in Pennsylvania. Mr. Ginter, himself, did not claim that he was the discoverer, because *"he had heard of stone coal over in Wyoming."*

Mr. Rapsher is certainly mistaken when he says that historians differ as to whether Philip Ginter was the first discoverer or not. No, they do not differ. All historians agree that Mr. Ginter discovered coal in what is now Carbon county, in 1791, and that *he was not the first discoverer of anthracite coal in Pennsylvania.* Ill informed people may think he was, but intelligent people know better. Mr. Rapsher states that the discovery of coal a hundred years ago the first of next September (1891), was the inception of the Lehigh Coal and Navigation Company, and was the beginning of the anthracite coal traffic in Pennsylvania. The Lehigh Coal and Navigation Company was incorporated February 13, 1822, and if its inception was in 1791, it took a long time to be born—even thirty-one years. The beginning of the coal trade was not on the Lehigh, but was on the Susquehanna, and commenced in 1807. Do not let this be forgotten. Senator Green thinks "we ought to have a discoverer of coal." "Whether it is Mr. Ginter, or somebody else, makes very little difference to (him) me." Most noble senator; you certainly do not speak the words of truth and soberness. In a work gotten up by the Central Railroad of New Jersey, in 1891, I read the following: "Mauch Chunk is in the very heart of the anthracite coal regions, and is also the *birthplace in America* of the Black Diamonds." Considering that coal was discovered on the Susquehanna in 1762, and on Bear Mountain, nine miles west of Mauch Chunk, in 1791, Mauch Chunk is a queer kind of a birthplace. It goes on the principle, claim everything for the Lehigh.

What surprises me, is that nothing in particular is claimed for the Schuylkill region. About all the worthies who make up tables and pyramids are Pottsville gentlemen, like Bannan, Daddow, Sheafer, *et al.* They are probably not familiar with the history of the state, and least of all, with the coal trade and its beginning in the Wyoming region. With a new generation of better informed gentlemen Wyoming will probably have justice done her in the future.

region in 1842, as shipping by canal forty-seven thousand three hundred and forty-six tons—a surely good commencement, if true, of the first year's business on the canal. Our canal was opened in 1831. In 1830 the North Branch Canal was completed to the Nanticoke dam. The first boat, "The Wyoming," was built by Hon. John Koons, at Shickshinny. It was launched and towed to Nanticoke, where she was laden with ten tons of anthracite coal, a quantity of flour and other articles. Her destination was Philadelphia. The North Branch canal being new, and filling slowly with water, "The Wyoming" passed through the Nanticoke *chute* and thence down the river to Northumberland, where she entered the Susquehanna division of the Pennsylvania canal, and proceeded, with considerable difficulty, by the way of the Union and Schuylkill canals to Philadelphia. "The Wyoming" received in that city fifteen tons of dry goods, and commenced her return trip; was frozen up in the ice and snow at New Buffalo, in January, 1831. The voyage of "The Wyoming" was attended with many difficulties and detentions, and embraced a period of upwards of three months. The second boat, "The Luzerne," was built by Captain Derrick Bird, on the river bank opposite Wilkes-Barre. She was laden with coal which was conveyed to Philadelphia, whence she returned with a cargo of merchandise, arriving at the Nanticoke dam in July, 1831. The pyramid starts us in 1846 with five thousand eight hundred and eighty-six tons by the Lehigh railroad. The mistake about this is that the Lehigh & Susquehanna railroad was completed in 1843. These figures from the pyramid are by Benjamin Bannan, and taken from "Coal, Iron and Oil." Pearce, in his "Annals of Luzerne County," says: "The completion of the Lehigh & Susquehanna railroad in 1843, connecting Wilkes-Barre with White Haven, promised another outlet to market for Wyoming coal. These improvements, together with the discovery of the methods of generating steam on boats, and of smelting iron in furnaces by the use of anthracite, created a great and increasing demand for coal in all quarters of the state, and in the seaports of the country generally." Let us take another pyramid, that of P. W. Sheafer, in the "Coal Regions of America." He has the old "chestnut" of the "commencement of the coal trade" in 1820, on the Lehigh, with three hundred and sixty-five tons. He lets us in with the "Wyoming and State Canals, Lykens Valley railroad," in 1834, with forty-three thousand seven hundred tons, and the Lehigh & Susquehanna railroad in 1846. This pyramid business should be reconstructed. The stereotype should be destroyed. The apex should be an inch longer and given to Wyoming. The commencement of the coal trade belongs to her, and there is no excuse for ignorance or carelessness in the matter. *She had knowledge of coal twenty-nine years, and had burned it twenty-two years before it was discovered on the Lehigh*, and she put her knowledge to good use. When the time came the Yankees took their coal to market and *sold* it. None of their coal was thrown into the street as worthless. Under the instruction given by the Yankees to the purchasers they found that coal *would* burn, and nobody laughed at them for making investments in "black stones."

Philip Ginter discovered coal in the Lehigh region in 1791, on the Matchunk or Bear Mountain, about nine miles west of the site of Mauch Chunk. Mr. Ginter tells his own story, as follows:

"When I first came to these mountains some years ago, I built a cabin on the east side of the mountain, and managed, by hunting and trapping, to support my family in a rough way. Deer and bears were pretty thick, and during the hunting season meat was plentiful, but sometimes we ran short of that, and frequently were hard up for such necessaries, as could only be purchased with the produce of the hunter. One day, after a poor season, when we were on short allowance, I had unusually bad luck, and was on my way home empty handed and disheartened, tired and wet with the rain which commenced falling, when I struck my foot against a stone and drove it on before me. It was nearly dusk, but light enough remained to show me that it was black and shiny. *I had heard of 'stone coal' over in Wyoming, and had frequently pried into rocks in hopes of finding it.* When I saw the black rock I knew it must be stone coal, and on looking round I discovered black dirt and a great many pieces of stone coal under the roots of a tree that had been blown down. I took pieces of this coal home with me, and the next day carried them to Colonel Jacob Weiss, at Fort Allen (Weissport). A few days after this Colonel Weiss sent for me and offered to pay me for my discovery if I would tell him where the coal was found. I accordingly offered to show him the place if he would get me a small tract of land and water power for a saw mill I had in view. This he readily promised and afterwards performed. The place was found and a quarry opened in the coal mountain. In a few years the discovery made hundreds of fortunes, but I may say it ruined me, for my land was taken from me by a man who said he owned it before I did, and now I am still a poor man."

Mr. F. E. Saward in The Coal Trade for 1891, states that the Northern Anthracite Coal Field is the largest anthracite basin in the world. It has long been known as the Wyoming. Its coal production since 1860 is as follows:

```
1860 . . . . . . . . . . . . . 2,914,817 tons.
1870 . . . . . . . . . . . . . 7,974,666   "
1880 . . . . . . . . . . . . .11,419,270   "
1890 . . . . . . . . . . . . .18,657,694   "
```

To mine this coal requires the services of over 50,000 men and boys, and this number is steadily increasing rather than diminishing.

The total amount of anthracite coal mined in 1890, was 35,865,000 tons. Thus it will be seen that the Wyoming region produces 52 per cent. of the total anthracite production. The Schuylkill region in 1890, produced 10,867,821 tons, or 30.31 per cent., and the Lehigh region, the same year, produced 6,329,658 tons, or 17.65 per cent., and the Wyoming region, as we have seen, produced 18,657,694 tons, or 52.04 per cent.

We must disagree with Mr. Saward, as *every body else does who has any knowledge of the subject*, when he states that "the tables compiled by Prof. P. W. Sheafer, for the years 1820 to 1868, inclusive, * * * have been adopted as the most correct so far as a report of the output is concerned." (See our remarks in regard to Mr. Sheafer's tables in another place). Mr. Saward says, further: "The first means of transporting coal from the (Wyoming) coal field was by the Delaware & Hudson Canal, from Honesdale, Pa., to Rondout, N. Y., opened in 1829." This is certainly ignorance of the first water. Please remember that the coal trade on the Susquehanna river commenced in 1807, and constantly grew in importance. We have given in another place the trade up to 1820. Stewart Pearce's Annals of Luzerne County gives the following: "In 1823, Colonel W. Lee and George Cahoon, leased the Stivers mines in Newport, fourteen feet vein, and employed Timothy Mansfield to mine and deliver one thousand tons of coal into arks at Lee's Ferry. This coal was sold at Columbia, Pa." Mr. Pearce says, further: "From 1823 to 1829, the Susquehanna coal trade increased with considerable rapidity." Again Mr. Pearce says: "A coal bed was opened by Calvin Stockbridge in 1828, and during three years he sent about two thousand tons down the Susquehanna in arks." Mr. Saward states, further: "Shipments of coal from the Wilkes-Barre district began in 1846, via. the Lehigh and Susquehanna Railroad, and the Lehigh Canal, and later by the

Lehigh Valley Railroad." We are sorry, exceedingly sorry that Mr. Saward states that "shipments of coal from the Wilkes-Barre district began in 1846." Why, Mr. Sheafer does better than this. He starts us in the Wyoming region in 1842, as shipping by canal. It is true our canal was opened in 1831, but Messrs. Sheafer and Saward were not aware of this fact, or they would agree on their table. Mr. Pearce, in his Annals, states that there was 41,210 tons of coal shipped from the Wyoming valley, by the North Branch Canal, South, in 1841.

In 1842 . . . . 47,346 tons.
" 1843 . . . . 57,740 "
" 1844 . . . . 114,906 "
" 1845 . . . . 178,401 "
" 1846 . . . . 166,923 "

Both Messrs. Sheafer and Saward agree that the Lehigh and Susquehanna Railroad was opened in 1846. The Lehigh and Susquehanna railroad was completed in 1843, but Messrs. Sheafer and Saward were not aware of this fact. *All we ask is that justice be done to the Wyoming region. We are entitled to it and expect it.* Mr. Saward further states, that in 1850 the Pennsylvania Coal Company began operations (which is correct); four years later the D. L. & W. R. R. Co. began mining and shipping coal. The Lackawanna coal field was opened to the coal trade in 1851 (not 1854), by the construction of the northern division of the D., L. & W. R. R. Co.

William Hooker Smith, M. D., removed from the province of New York, to Wilkes-Barre, in 1772, where he purchased land in 1774. His mind active, keen and ready, looked beyond the ordinary conceptions of his day, as is shown by his purchased right, in 1791, to dig iron ore and stone coal in Pittston, long before the character of coal as a heating agent in this country was understood, and the same year that the hunter, Ginter, accidently discovered "black stones" on Bear Mountain. These purchases, attracting no other notice than general ridicule, were made in Exeter, Plymouth, Pittston, Providence and Wilkes-Barre, between 1791–8. The first was made July 1, 1791, of Mr. Scott of Pittston, who, for the sum of five shillings, Pennsylvania money, sold "one-half of any minerals, ores of iron, or other metal which he, the said Smith, or his heirs and assigns, may discover on the hilly lands of the said John Scott, by the red spring." Of others, the language of the purchase was as follows: "The privilege to dig, delve and raze the ore, or mineral of stone coal, or iron ore on my land, free and clear, by William Hooker Smith."

It is impossible, at this date, to state who was the first person to discover that anthracite coal could be used for domestic purposes, but the weight of authority seems to be that Oliver Evans was the person. In a letter written by him to Jacob Cist, Esq., he says: "Being required to give my opinion of the qualities of the Lehi coals, I do certify to those whom it may concern, that I have experienced the use of them in a close stove and also in a fire place that may be closed and opened at pleasure, so contracted as to cause a brisk current of air to pass up through a small contracted grate on which they were laid. I find them more difficult to be kindled than the Virginia coal, yet a small quantity of dry wood laid on the grate under them is sufficient to ignite them, which being done they continue to burn while a sufficient quantity be added to keep up the combustion, occasionally stirring them to shake down the ashes. They, however, require no more attention than other coal, and consume away, leaving only a very light and white colored ashes; producing a greater degree of heat than any other coal that I am acquainted with, perhaps, in proportion to their weight, they being much the heaviest. They produce no smoke, contain no sulphur, and when well ignited exhibit a vivid, bright appearance, all which render them suitable for warming rooms. And as they do not corrode mettle as much as other coals, they will probably be the more useful for steam engines, breweries, distilleries, smelting of metals, drying malt, &c. But the furnaces will require to be properly constructed, with a grate contracted to a small space through which the air is to pass up through the coal, permitting none to pass above them into the flue of the chimney until they are well ignited, when the doors of the stove or furnace or close fire place may be thrown open to enjoy the benefits of light and radiant heat in the front. A very small quantity of them is not sufficient to keep up the combustion; they require nearly a cubic foot to make a very warm fire, consuming about half a bus. in about fourteen hours. "OLIVER EVANS.

"Philadelphia, February 15, 1803."

It a letter to Jacob Cist, Esq., Frederick Graff also writes as follows: "Having made a trial of the Lehi coal some time in the year 1802 at the Pennsylvania bank, in the large stove, I found them to answer for that purpose exceeding well. They give an excellent heat and burn lively. It is my opinion they are nearly equal to double the quantity of any other coal brought to this market for durability; of course less labour is required in attending the fire. Mr. Davis, superintendent of the water works, has also made a trial of them for the boiler of the engine imployed in that work, and has found them to answer well. It must be observed a draft is necessary when first kindled. For the use of familys the fire place can be so constructed, with a small expense, as to have the sufficient draft required. My opinion is they will be found cheaper than wood. They burn clean. No smoke or sulphur is observed, or any dirt flying when stirred, which is a great objection to all other coal for family use. If the chimneys for the burning of those coal

are properly constructed, and a trial made, I am well convinced that most of the citizens of Philadelphia would give them preference to wood. "FRED'K GRAFF,
"*Clerk of the Water Works of Philadelphia.*
"Phila., May 1, 1805."

The originals of these letters are in the possession of our Society.

Jacob Cist, at the time these letters were written, if not an actual resident of this city at that time, was a very frequent visitor. In 1807 he married Sarah Hollenback, daughter of Judge Hollenback.

At an early day his attention was attracted towards the uses of anthracite coal. He was a boy of ten years when his father experimented on the Lehigh coal, and he might possibly have seen him at work. He must often have heard his father conversing with Colonel Weiss (the uncle of Jacob Cist), both in Philadelphia and Bethlehem, on the feasibility of opening their mines and making a market for the Lehigh coal, long before he was old enough to appreciate the importance of the undertaking or the disadvantages under which these pioneers of the coal trade labored in persuading people of the practicability of using stone coal as a fuel.

Jacob Cist was undoubtedly the first person to burn anthracite coal in our city. The letter of Oliver Evans, with its perfect description of burning anthracite coal in a grate or stove, accomplished the result. No better description could be given nowadays to those unfamiliar with coal for fuel than the letter of Mr. Evans. Mr. Cist was an enterprising citizen, perfectly familiar and interested in coal. He made the "experiment" and found that it would "answer the purpose of fuel, making a cleaner and better fire at less expense than burning wood in the common way." As early as the year 1805 he conceived the plan of manufacturing a mineral black for printers' ink, leather lacquer, blacking, &c., from the Lehigh coal and the results of his experiments were secured to him by patent in 1808. This patent was considered to be worth upwards of five thousand dollars, but a number of law suits arising from a constant infringement of it by manufacturers so annoyed Mr. Cist that he was glad to dispose of it for a less sum. It is said that after the destruction of the patent office records by fire some one else took out a patent for the same idea and is now working under it. In the early days he made a study of our adjacent coal fields, especially at the mines of the Smith Brothers at Plymouth, and the old Lord Butler opening.

We believe that from 1803 anthracite coal was used for domestic purposes in this city. We have not before us the population of Wilkes-Barre at that time, but in 1820 she had a population of seven hundred and thirty-two. In 1803 the population probably did not exceed three hundred. These letters, written to one of her citizens, would excite comment and would be talked over by the entire population, men, women and children. The social standard of her citizens at that time was perfect equality. There were no ranks or grades. The apprentice, the laborer, the physician, the merchant and the lawyer were on speaking and visiting terms. As another writer has said, in speaking of the early history of coal : "Such was the theme of universal rejoicing throughout the valley that the event was discussed at every fireside, the topic went with the people to church, and was diffused throughout the congregation at large by common assent; it entered for a while into all conversations at home; it silenced every adverse criticism, as it gave the signal for long and mutual congratulations * * * where friend and foe alike acquiesced in the truth that Wyoming was freighted with infinite fortune." Coal up to this time had been mined by farmers and blacksmiths for their own use. In 1805 Abraham Williams, the pioneer miner, made his appearance in the *Federalist*, published at Wilkes-Barre, with the following advertisement :

"The subscriber takes this method of informing the public that he understands miners work. He has worked at it the greater part of twenty-three years in the mines of Wales, one year and a half in Schuyler's copper mines in New Jersey and three years in Ogden's in the same state. If any body thinks there is any ore on his lands, or wants to sink wells, blow rock or stones, he understands it wet or dry, on the ground or under the ground. He will work by the day or by the solid foot or yard, or by the job, at reasonable wages, for country produce.

> "He works cheap for country produce,
> But cash I think he wont refuse.
> Money is good for many uses,
> Despise me not nor take me scorn,
> Because I am a Welshman by my born,
> Now I am a true American,
> With every good to every man."
>
> "Abraham Williams."

Doctor Thomas C. James of Philadelphia, in *Hazard's Register*, gives an account of a visit that he made in 1804 to the Lehigh coal region. He closes his article as follows: "The operations and success of the present Lehigh Coal and Navigation Company must be well known to the country; the writer will therefore close this communication by stating that he commenced burning the anthracite coal in the winter of 1804, and has continued its use ever since, believing, from his own experience of its utility, that it would ultimately become the general fuel of this as well as other cities."

Hon. Samuel Breck was a prominent citizen of Philadelphia. "His Recollections," with passages from his note books, 1771–1862, were edited by H. E. Scudder, and published by Porter & Coates in 1877. It contains this passage, among others:

"December 9, 1807. This morning I rode to Philadelphia and purchased a newly invented iron grate calculated for coal, in which I mean to use that fuel if it answers my expectations."

"Dec. 26, 1807. By my experiment on coal fuel I find that one fire place will burn from three to three and a half bushels per week in hard weather and about two and a half in moderate weather. This averages three bushels for twenty-five weeks (the period of burning fire in parlors). Three times twenty-five gives seventy-five bushels for a single hearth, which, at forty-five cents, is thirty-three dollars and seventy-five cents, more than equal to six cords of oak wood at five dollars and fifty cents, and is, by consequence, no economy; but at thirty-three cents per bushel, which is the usual summer price, it will do very well."

The next person whom it is said burned coal in grates in the early days of coal fuel was Hon. Jesse Fell, of this city. He was a blacksmith in his early days, and had used coal in a nailery as early as 1788. He made the following entry on the last leaf of a book entitled "Illustrations of Masonry by William Preston—Alexandria—Printed by Cottom & Stewart, and sold at their Book Stores in Alexandria and Fredericksburg, 1804." On the fly leaf in Judge Fell's handwriting is the following: "Jesse Fell's Book, February 15th, 1808."

"February 11, of Masonry 5808. Made the *experment* of burning the common stone coal of this Valley in a grate, in a common fire place, in my house, and find it will answer the purpose of fuel, making a clearer and better fire at less expence than burning wood in the common way.

"JESSE FELL.

"Borough of Wilkes-Barre, Feb'y 18, 1808."

We do not believe, as some do, that Jesse Fell was the first person to burn anthracite coal in a grate in this county. He makes no claim in the above that he was. Those who make that claim, do so for the following reasons:

1. The entry as stated above.

2. That he "constructed a grate of green hickory saplings and placed it in a large fire place in his bar room, and filled it with broken coal. A quantity of dry wood was placed *under the grate* and set on fire, and the flame spreading through the coal it soon ignited, and before the wooden grate was consumed the success of the experiment was fully demonstrated."

3. That Hon. Thomas Cooper, president judge of the courts of Luzerne county, "became very angry to find that he had been superseded in the discovery, and he walked the floor muttering to himself, 'that it was strange an illiterate man like Fell' (which was not true) 'should discover what he had tried in vain to find out.'"

To these we answer:

1. There is no claim in the entry that Judge Fell was the first person to burn anthracite in a grate. He states he made the "*experment.*" It is very strange that an "experiment" should be made after a fact had been fully demonstrated. We think that he burned coal in a grate as early as 1803, as that was the time when, we believe, coal was first burned successfully in grates in Wilkes-Barre. If he did not he was certainly behind the times. We do not think that he would wait five years to make the "experiment" after his friend Jacob Cist received letters from Messrs. Evans & Graff. We also think that if he made the experiment in 1808 it would be published in *The Luzerne Federalist*. Mr. Miner would never slight his friend in that way. We think this entry was made at a date subsequent to 1808.

V. L. Maxwell, in his lectures on Mineral Coal, says: "At that day the Hon. Charles Miner was publishing in this town *The Luzerne Federalist*, the only newspaper then printed in this part of the state. I have had the pleasure of examining its files, but I find nothing published in 1808 respecting coal." It was rather late in 1808 to make an "experiment" after the fact had been fully demonstrated by

Messrs. Evans, Graff, Davis, James and Breck, several years before. The coal trade was opened by the Smith Brothers in 1807, and their first shipment was made in that year, and the year after was certainly a bad time to make the "experiment" of burning coal in a grate.

2. We do not believe that a blacksmith, as Mr. Fell was, would "construct a grate of green hickory saplings," and make the experiment of burning coal in it. A bar iron grate would be so much easier to make and would prove more satisfactory. We are not foolish enough to think, with our knowledge of coal, that a quantity of dry wood placed under a grate of green hickory and set on fire would prove the experiment of burning coal in a grate. The experiment, it seems to us, would be to dry the green hickory and then consume it and leave the coal down without much ignition.

3. Judge Cooper was born in London in 1759, and came to this country in 1795, and was, therefore, thirty-six years of age when he came to America. It is probable that before he came to this country he never saw any other fuel than coal, and that burned in grates. It is not at all likely that he would become very angry to find that he had been superseded in the discovery. It was not a new thing to him and he had no discovery to make.

Mrs. Hannah C. Abbott, a resident of this city, the widow of John Abbott, and daughter of Hon. Cornelius Courtright, was born February 7, 1797, in Wilkes-Barre (now Plains) township. Her father's farm adjoined that of Daniel Gore, whom we have seen, burned coal in his blacksmith shop as early as 1769. She has been familiar with coal since her earliest recollection, having seen Mr. Gore burn it in his blacksmith shop, and in a grate in his cellar kitchen. She has no remembrance as to who the first person was who burned coal in a grate, but is certain that it was not Mr. Fell, as she never heard the claim made until she was grown up. In 1808 she was eleven years of age, and if Mr. Fell burned coal in a grate at that time she would certainly remember it, as her father and Mr. Fell were particular friends, and both belonged to the same political party. Mrs. Abbott, notwithstanding her advanced age, is in the full possession of all her mental faculties, and is about the only person living who has a perfect knowledge of the very early coal trade of the valley.

If Judge Fell made the discovery that coal could be burned in grates successfully, he should have the honor due all persons who make valuable discoveries, and we would be the last person to rob him of his honors. But in the light we have to-day we must say that he was not the first person, but that in 1808 coal was a common fuel in this city, and was burned by all persons who had not wood in profusion. Improbable assertion, unreasonable conjectures and old wives' fables are not the best evidence that Judge Fell was the first person to burn anthracite coal in a grate in this city or anywhere else.

The following authorities, in part, have been consulted in preparing this paper:

Buck, Wm. J., Article by, in Report of the Transactions of the Pennsylvania State Agricultural Society.
Chance, H. M., Report of the Mining Methods and Appliances used in the Anthracite Coal Fields—Second Geological Survey of Pennsylvania.
Chapman, I. A., History of Wyoming.
Daddow & Bannon, Coal, Iron and Oil.
Encyclopædia Brittanica.
Hazard, Samuel, Register of Pennsylvania.
Hollister, H., History of the Lackawanna Valley.
Hoyt, H. M., Brief of a Title in the Seventeen Townships.
Kulp, Geo. B., Families of the Wyoming Valley.
Macaulay, Lord, History of England.
Macfarlane, James, Coal Regions of America.
Maxwell, V. L., Mineral Coal.
Miner, Charles, History of Wyoming.
Pearce, Stewart, Annals of Luzerne County.
Plumb, H. B., History of Hanover.
Rees, Abraham, Cyclopædia of Arts, Science and Literature.
Saward, Frederick E., The Coal Trade.
Watson, John F., Annals of Philadelphia and Pennsylvania in the Olden Time.
Wright, Hendrick B., Historical Sketches of Plymouth.

SABBATH—SUNDAY.

SUNDAY LEGISLATION.

SABBATH—SUNDAY.

SUNDAY LEGISLATION.

In the beginning, after the Almighty created the heavens and the earth, and all the host of them, He rested on the seventh day from all His work which He had made. And God blessed the seventh day and sanctified it, because that in it He had rested from all His work which He had made. This was the commencement of the Sabbath day. The Lord Jehovah blessed the day, but there was no injunction to man to keep it holy, unless implied from the blessing and sanctification.

Eusebius of Cæsarea (bishop from 315–340 A. D.) discusses the question of the observance of the Sabbath in his Commentary on Psalm xcii (xci of his catalogue). He takes the ground of Justin and Irenæus, that the early patriarchs knew no Sabbaths, and were justified without the observance of them. He says: "The just and pious men who were before Moses neither knew nor observed Sabbath days. Neither Abraham, nor Isaac, nor Jacob, nor they who were before them, seem to have known the Sabbath." He argues that man's true rest, and therefore his true Sabbath, is to be found in the contemplation of God, and that Moses, dealing with shadows and symbols, gave the people a fixed day, that on this at least they might be free for meditation on divine things. The Jewish Sabbaths, however, became false Sabbaths, and God said He could not endure them. Wherefore the Word, by the new covenant, transferred the feast of the Sabbath to the rising of the light, and gave us the image of the true rest, namely, the saving day, the Lord's Day, the first day of light, on which the Saviour of the world, having conquered death, entered on a Sabbath becoming to God, and a most blissful rest. Whatever things it was fitting to do on the Sabbath we have transferred to the Lord's Day, because it has precedence, is first, and is more honorable than the Jewish Sabbath. (Com. on Psa. xci: 2, 3.)

The Jews appear to have forgotten the first of all the commandments of God: "Thou camest down also upon Mount Sinai and spakest with them from heaven, and gavest them right judgments and true laws, good statutes and commandments: and *madest known unto them thy holy Sabbath*, and commandest them precepts, statutes and laws, *by the hand of Moses thy servant.*" (Nehemiah ix: 13, 14.)

Centuries pass; the Israelites are about to leave Egypt, the passover is instituted, "and this day shall be unto you for a memorial; and ye shall keep it a feast to the Lord throughout your generations: ye shall keep it a feast by an ordinance for ever. Seven days shall ye eat unleavened bread; even the first day ye shall put away leaven out of your houses: for whosoever eateth leavened bread from the first day until the seventh day, that soul shall be cut off from Israel. And in the first day there shall be a holy convocation, and in the seventh day there shall be a holy convocation to you; no manner of work shall be done in them, save that which every man must eat, that only may be done of you." (Exodus xii: 14–16). This is the first place where we meet with the account of an assembly collected for the mere purpose of religious worship. Such assemblies are called holy convocations, which is a very appropriate appellation for a religious assembly; they were called together by the express command of God, and were to be employed in a work of holiness.

Four weeks and more pass, the children of Israel are in the wilderness, manna is sent down from heaven. And it came to pass that on the sixth day they gathered twice as much bread, two omers for one man, and all the rulers of the congregation came and told Moses. And he said unto them, This is that which the Lord hath said, to-morrow is the rest of the holy Sabbath unto the Lord; bake that ye will bake to-day, and seethe that ye will seethe, and that which remaineth over lay up for you to be kept until the morning. * * * And Moses said 'eat that to-day, for to-day is a Sabbath unto the Lord, to-day ye shall not find it in the field. Six days ye shall gather it, but on the seventh day, which is the Sabbath, in it there shall be none. And it came to pass that there went out some of the people on the seventh day for to gather and they found none. And the Lord said unto Moses: How long refuse ye to keep my commandments and my laws? See for that the Lord hath given you the Sabbath, therefore He giveth you on the sixth day the bread of two days; abide ye every man in his place; let no man go out of his place on the seventh day. So the people rested on the seventh day. Two weeks and more pass and the Almighty is again heard; then a positive command goes forth from the smoking top of Mount Sinai. Remember the Sabbath day to keep it holy. Six days shalt thou labor and do all thy work, but the seventh day is the Sabbath of the Lord thy God, in it thou shall not do any work, * * * for in six days the Lord made heaven and earth, the sea and all that in them is, and rested the seventh day; wherefore the Lord blessed the seventh day and hallowed it. Here the time in which man shall work and in which he shall not is fixed by Deity, himself, in a manner too solemn to be forgotten or disregarded. It was pronounced with the voice of a loud trumpet, midst the lightnings and the quakings of the mount. And Moses gathered all the congregation of the children of Israel together and said unto them, these are the words which the Lord hath commanded hat ye should do them. Six days shall work be done, but on the seventh day there shall be to you a holy day, a Sabbath of rest to the Lord; whosoever doeth work therein shall be put to death. Thus was proclaimed the first punishment for a violation of the Sabbath day. And while the children of Israel were in the wilderness they found a man that gathered sticks upon the Sabbath day. And they that found him gathering sticks brought him unto Moses and Aaron, and unto all the congregation. And they put him in ward because it was not declared what should be done to him. And the Lord said unto Moses—the man shall be surely put to death; all the congregation shall stone him with stones without the camp. And all the congregation brought him without the camp and stoned him with stones, and he died as the Lord commanded Moses.

The stoning of the Bible and of the Talmud was not as commonly supposed—a pell-mell casting of stones at a criminal. The manner was as follows: The criminal was conducted to an elevated place, divested of his attire, if a man, and then hurled to the ground below. The height of the eminence from which he was thrown was always more than fifteen feet; the higher, within certain limits, the better. The violence of the concussion caused death by dislocating the spinal cord. The elevation was not, however, to be so high as to greatly disfigure the body. This was a tender point with the Jews; man was created in God's image, and it was not permitted to desecrate the temple shaped by heaven's own hand. The first of the witnesses who had testified against the condemned man acted as executioner, in accordance with Deut. xvii: 7. If the convict fell face downward, he was turned on his back. If he was not quite dead, a stone so heavy as to require two persons to carry it, was taken to the top of the eminence whence he had been thrown, the second of the witnesses then hurled the stone so as to fall upon the culprit below. This process, however, was seldom necessary, the semi-stupefied condition of the condemned, and the height from which he was cast insuring, in the generality of cases, instant death. Previous to the carrying into effect a sentence of death, a death-draught, as it was called, was administered to the unfortunate victim. The beverage was composed of myrrh and frankincense (*lebana*), in a cup of vinegar or light wine. It produced a kind of stupefaction, a semi-conscious condition of mind and body, rendering the convict indifferent to his fate and scarcely sensible to pain. As soon as the culprit had partaken of the stupefying draught the execution took place.

The later Jewish Sabbath, observed in accordance with the rules of the Scribes, was a very peculiar institution, and formed one of the most marked distinctions between the Hebrews and other nations, as appears in a striking way from the fact that on this account, alone, the Romans found themselves compelled to exempt the Jews from all military service. The rules of the Scribes enumerated thirty nine main kinds of work forbidden on the Sabbath, and each of these prohibitions gave rise to new subtleties. Jesus's disciples, for example, who plucked ears of corn in passing through a field on the holy day, had, according to Rabbinical casuistry, violated the third of the thirty-nine rules, which forbade harvesting; and in healing the sick Jesus, himself, broke the rule that a sick man should not receive medical aid on the Sabbath, unless his life was in danger. In fact, as our Lord puts it, the Rabbinical theory seemed to be that the Sabbath was not made for man, but man for the Sabbath, the observance of which was so much an end in itself that the rules prescribed for it did not require to be justified by appeal to any larger principle of religion or humanity. The precepts of the law were valuable in the eyes of the Scribes, because they were the seal of Jewish particularism, the barrier erected between the world at large and the exclusive community of Jehovah's grace. For this purpose the most arbitrary precepts were the most effective, and none were more so than the complicated rules of Sabbath observance. The ideal of the Sabbath, which all these rules aimed at realizing, was absolute rest from everything that could be called work; and even the exercise of those offices of humanity which the strictest Christian Sabbatarians regard as a service to God, and therefore as specially appropriate to His day, was looked on as work. To save life was allowed, but only because danger to life "superseded the Sabbath." In like manner the special ritual at the temple prescribed for the Sabbath by the Pentateuchal law was not regarded as any part of the hallowing of the sacred day, on the contrary, the rule was that in this regard "Sabbath was not kept in the sanctuary." Strictly speaking, therefore, the Sabbath was neither a day of relief to toiling humanity, nor a day appointed for public worship; the positive duties of its observance were to wear one's best clothes, eat, drink and be glad. (Justified from lviii Isaiah: 13, 14).

A more directly religious element, it is true, was introduced by the practice of attending the synagogue service, but it is to be remembered that this service was primarily regarded not as an act of worship, but as a meeting for instruction in the law. So far, therefore, as the Sabbath existed for any end outside itself, it was an institution to help every Jew to learn the law. That the old Hebrew Sabbath was quite different from the Rabbinical Sabbath, is demonstrated in the trenchant criticism which Jesus directed against the latter. (Matthew xii: 1-14; Mark ii: 27). The general position which He takes up, that "the Sabbath is made for man, and not man for the Sabbath," is only a special application of the wider principle, that the law is not an end in itself, but a help towards the realization in life of the great ideal of love to God and man, which is the sum of all true religion. But Jesus further maintains that this view of the law, as a whole, and the interpretation of the Sabbath law which it involves, can be historically justified from the old testament. And, in this connexion, He introduces two of the main methods to which historical criticism of the old testament has recurred in modern times. He appeals to the oldest history, rather than to the Pentateuchal code, as proving that the later conception of the law was unknown in ancient times (Matthew xii: 3-4), and to the exceptions to the Sabbath law which the Scribes, themselves, allowed in the interests of worship (verse 5), or humanity (verse 11), as showing that the Sabbath must originally have been devoted to purposes of worship and humanity, and was not always the purposeless, arbitrary thing which the schoolmen made it to be. The Sabbath exercised a twofold influence on the early Christian church. On the one hand, the weekly celebration of the resurrection on the Lord's day could not have arisen, except in a circle that already knew the week as a sacred division of time, and, moreover, the manner in which the Lord's day was observed, was directly influenced by the synagogue service. On the other hand, the Jewish Christians continued to keep the Sabbath like other points of the old law. Eusebius remarks that the Ebionites observed both the Sabbath and the Lord's day, and this practice obtained, to some extent, in much wider circles, for the Apostolical Constitutions recommend that the Sabbath shall be kept as a memorial feast of the creation, as well as the Lord's day; as a memorial of the resurrection. The festal character of the Sabbath was long recognized in a modified form in the Eastern church, by a prohibition of fasting on that day, which was also a point in the Jewish Sabbath law. On the other hand Paul had quite distinctly laid down from the first days of Gentile Chistianity that the Jewish Sabbath was not binding on Christians (Romans xiv: 5; Galations iv: 10; Col. ii: 16), and controversy with Judaizers led in process of time to direct condemnation of those who still kept the Jewish day. According to all the four evangelists the resurrection of our Lord took place on the first day of the week after His crucifixion, and the fourth Gospel describes a second appearance to His disciples as having occurred eight days afterwards. Apart from this central fact of the Christian faith, the Pentecostal outpouring of the Spirit seven weeks later, described in Acts ii, cannot have failed to give an additional sacredness to the day in the eyes of the earliest converts. Whether the primitive church in Jerusalem had any special mode of observing it in its daily meetings held in the temple we cannot tell, but as there is no doubt that in these gatherings the recurrence of the Sabbath was marked by appropriate Jewish observances, so it is not improbable that the worship on the first day of the week had also some distinguishing feature. Afterwards, at all events, when Christianity had been carried to other places where, from the nature of the case, daily meetings for worship were impossible, the first day of the week was everywhere set apart for this purpose. Thus, Acts xx: 7 shows that the disciples in Troas met weekly on the first day of the week for exhortation and the breaking of bread (I Corinthians xvi: 2); implies, at least, some observance of the day, and the solemn commemorative character it had very early acquired is strikingly indicated by an incidental expression of the writer of the Apocalypse, i: 10, who, for the first time, gives it that name—The Lord's day—by which it is almost invariably referred to by all writers of the century immediately succeeding apostolic times. Among the indications of the nature and universality of its observance during this period, may be mentioned the precept in the (recently discovered) Teaching of the Apostles (chap. xiv). "And on the Lord's day of the Lord come together and break bread and give thanks after confessing your transgressions, that your sacrifice may be pure." Ignatius speaks of those whom he addresses as no longer Sabbatizing, but living in the observance of the Lord's day, on which also our life sprang up again. Justin Martyr, during the reign of Antonius Pius, 138–161, says of the weekly meetings of the Christians: "And on the day called Sunday, all who live in the cities or in the country gather together to one place, and the memoirs of the apostles or the writings of the prophets are read, as long as time permits; then when the reader has ceased, the president verbally instructs and exhorts to the imitation of these good things. * * * But Sunday is the day on which we hold our common assembly, because it is the first day on which God, having wrought a change in the darkness and matter, made the world; and Jesus Christ, our Saviour, on the same day rose from the dead; for He was crucified on the day before that of Saturn, and on the day after that of Saturn, which is the day of the sun, having appeared to His apostles and disciples, He taught them those things which we have submitted to you also for your consideration."

A new name now appears for the first day of the week which is not found in either the old or new Testament—Sunday; so called because this day was anciently dedicated to the sun as its worship. Sun worship was the worship of the greater part of the people of the East. We are reminded in God's word to take good heed unto ourselves lest thou lift up thine eyes to heaven, and when thou seest the sun, the moon and the stars shouldest be driven to worship them. (Deuteronomy iv: 19). This term Sunday, was afterwards adopted by Christian nations. It is also called the Lord's day, the first day of the week, the Sabbath. Sabbath—rest—day of rest—the day which God appointed to be observed as a day of rest from all secular labor or employment, for the study of His law and for praise, to be kept holy and to be consecrated to His service and worship. Sabbath is not strictly synonomous with

Sunday. Sunday is a mere name of a day. Sabbath is the name of an institution. Sunday is the Sabbath of the Christians. Saturday is the Sabbath of the Jews. It has been contended whether Sunday is a name that ought to be used by Christians. The words Sabbath and Lord's day, say some, are the only names mentioned in Scripture respecting this day. To call it Sunday is to set our wisdom before the wisdom of God, and to give that glory to a pagan idol, which is due to Him alone. The ancient Romans called it by this name, because, upon it, they worshipped the sun, and shall Christians keep up the memory of that which was highly displeasing to God by calling the Sabbath by that name rather than by either of those he hath appointed? The earliest civil law on the subject of Sunday is that of the Emperor Constantine, March 7, A. D. 321. The following is the decree: "On the venerable day of the sun let the magistrates and people residing in cities rest, and let all workshops be closed. In the country, however, persons engaged in the work of cultivation may freely and lawfully continue their pursuits, because it often happens that another day is not so suitable for grain-sowing or for vine-planting, lest by neglecting the proper moment for such operations, the bounty of heaven be lost." Constantine, at the time of issuing this decree, was a Pagan, who worshipped the god Apollo, whose sacred day was the first day of the week. Webster says: "Apollo was a deity among the Greeks and Romans, and worshipped under the name of Phœbus, the sun." Gibbon, in his "Decline and Fall of the Roman Empire," says: "The devotion of Constantine was more peculiarly directed to the genius of the sun, the Apollo of Greek and Roman mythology, and he was pleased to be represented with the symbols of the god of light and poetry. * * * The altars of Apollo were crowned with the votive offerings of Constantine, and the credulous multitude were taught to believe that the emperor was permitted to behold with mortal eyes the visible majesty of their tutelar deity. * * * The sun was universally celebrated as the invincible guide and protector of Constantine." Dr. Schaff, in his "History of the Christian Church," says: "Constantine enjoined the civil observance of Sunday, though not as *Dies Domini* (Lord's day), but as *Dies Solis*, day of the sun, in conformity to his worship of Apollo, and in company with his ordinance for the regular consulting of the *haruspice*. The edict of the sun's day was issued March 7, that for consulting the *haruspice* was issued the day following. This edict of March 8, concerned the inspection of the entrails of beasts as a means of foretelling future events. Let us examine a Roman army at the moment when it is preparing for battle. The consul orders a victim to be brought and strikes it with the axe, it falls, its entrails will indicate the will of the gods. An *haruspice* examines them, and if the signs are favorable the consul gives the signal for battle. The most skillful dispositions, the most favorable circumstances are of no account if the gods do not permit the battle. In 323, according to the opinion of Mosheim, Constantine made a profession of Christianity. Other writers give a later date. The Encyclopedia Brittanicæ says: "The notion of conversion in a sense of a real acceptance of the new religion, and a thorough rejection of the old, is inconsistent with the hesitating attitude in which he stood towards both. Much of this may indeed be due to motives of political expediency, but there is a good deal that cannot be so explained. Paganism must still have been an operative belief with the man who, down almost to the close of his life, retained so many heathen superstitions. He was, at best, only half heathen, half Christian, who could seek to combine the worship of Christ with the worship of Apollo, having the name of the one and the figure of the other impressed upon his coins. Dr. Schaff further says: "When at last, on his death bed, Constantine submitted to baptism, with the remark: 'Now let us cast away all duplicity,' he honestly admitted the conflict of two antagonistic principles which swayed his private character and public life." We herewith give a brief summary of the acts of Constantine, which seems to have a bearing on his inconsistent position as a pagan and a professed Christian:

A. D. 312, professed to have a vision of the cross. There is, however, no evidence that he ever spoke of such a thing before the year 322.

A. D. 313, issued the edict of Milan, stopping persecution on account of religion.

A. D. 321, March 7, issued a decree that certain classes abstain from labor on "the venerable day of the sun."

A. D. 321, March 8, issued a decree for consulting haruspices—a practice purely pagan.

A. D. 323, according to the opinion of Mosheim, made a profession of Christianity. Other writers give a later date.

A. D. 324, murdered Licinius, in violation of his solemn oath.

A. D. 325, convened the council of Nice, and presided over its deliberations.

A. D. 325, after the council, revoked the edict of Milan, and copied the penal regulations under which Diocletian had persecuted the Christians, and employed them in persecuting those who did not accept the Christian faith.

A. D. 326, murdered his son Crispus, and his nephew Licinius, and a great number of their friends.

A. D. 330, May 11, dedicated Constantinople to the virgin Mary.

A. D. 337, near the close of his life, was baptized into the Christian faith.

The first Sunday legislation was the product of that pagan conception so fully developed by the Romans, which made religion a department of the state. This was diametrically opposed to the genius of New Testament Christianity. It did not find favor in the church until Christianity had been deeply corrupted through the influence of gnosticism and kindred pagan errors. The Emperor Constantine issued the first Sunday edict by virtue of his power as *pontifex maximus* in all matters of religion, especially in the appointment of sacred days. This law was pagan in every particular.

Sunday legislation between the time of Constantine and the fall of the empire was a combination of the pagan, Christian and Jewish cults. Many other holidays—mostly pagan festivals baptized with new names and slightly modified—were associated in the same laws with Sunday.

In 321, Constantine declared it most unworthy of this day (Sunday), that it should be taken up with the strifes of the courts and the noxious contentions of suitors, and that it should rather be filled with good acts. This prohibition of law suits included arbitrations. Under the head of good acts are mentioned the emancipation of children, the manumission of slaves and the visitation of prisoners, to see that they were not cruelly treated. Later laws made further exceptions to the above. The judges were ordered by Theodosius (A. D. 408) to proceed against robbers, and especially against the Isaurian pirates at all times, not even excepting Easter or Lent; the reason given for this, being that otherwise the discovery of crimes expected from the torture of the robbers may be delayed and the pius hope is expressed that the High God will pardon the act being done on Sunday, because it tends to the safety of the many. There were numerous other exceptions for those which obtained as against the ante-Christian festivals of Rome were held still in force. Their object was to prevent a failure of justice in civil as well as criminal cases. Theodosius (A. D. 386), went further and extended the prohibition to all business as well as to litigation. In the same year he forbade shows on Sunday, "so that divine worship should not be mixed up with the slaughter of animals." Valentinian Theodosius and Arcadius (A. D. 392) forbade, on Sunday, the contests of the circus. Arcadius and Honorius added theatrical games and horse races, and Honorius and Theodosius (A. D. 409) added all pleasures. Leo and Anthenius go more into detail, and so make the prohibition of legal proceedings and of business more sweeping, and add, that in thus ordering a freedom from labor, they do not will that the day be given to immodest pleasures, and mention specially "theatrical representations," "games of the circus," and "tearful exhibitions of wild beasts." The Roman theatre was very different from the modern. Every citizen of Rome had a right to attend it without expense. Hence, instead of an audience few in numbers and of at least some culture, paying for their seats, there were often gathered at a Roman theatre 30,000 people of the very lowest and most brutal kind. This rabble—not the few—had to be pleased, and as the result taste soon degenerated. Purely dramatic representations gave way to clowns, boxers, jugglers, &c., and the theatres were soon polluted with the grossest indecencies, and the luxury of the stage, as the Romans delicately phrased it, drew down the loudest indignation of the reformers of a later day. The contests of the circus were the struggles to the death, often times, of the gladiators. The "tearful spectacles of wild beasts," were not simply fights between the beasts themselves, or their wholesale butchery by hired spearmen, but also fights between men and savage beasts, and yet further, the butchery of helpless men and women, cast bound to the animals to be destroyed by them. To the early Christians, with the memories of the days of Nero and others still fresh, these spectacles were especially hateful. They were condemned by the better class of Romans—the mere spectators; how much more then by those whose relatives, friends, leaders and fellow religionists had been compelled to act and suffer in them. These laws form the basis of the English legislation on this subject, and consequently of ours. They can easily be traced in these. Like the laws of their day, they deal with the concrete and do not lay down general rules. But the principle underlying them is easily seen. They forbid all labor or work on Sunday, except such as was essential, or at least highly conducive to the welfare, and which, in a broad sense, could be called necessary to the state and its citizens. Hence, the farmer could sow his seed and plant his vines, equally as the state could pursue robbers and pirates, and to prevent the loss of a right or the failure of justice, the private suitor could take legal proceedings, just as the state could take steps to prevent the escape of criminals. They prohibited pleasures which were, to a high degree, offensive to the taste and moral sense of the community. But they nowhere prohibited recreation or inoffensive pleasures or social enjoyments unless, indeed, the laws of Honorius and Theodosius severed from its connexion, be held to do this. This law, however, found no place in the Justinian code, and consequently did not last very long.

As it is through England that we have derived our laws on this, as on almost all subjects, we turn now to her legislation. Of the laws before the Norman conquest, the earliest is that of Ina or Ine, King of the West Saxons, in the year 692 or 693. It is as follows: "If a slave work on the Sunday by his lord's command, let him become a freeman, and let the lord pay thirty shillings for mulct. But if the slave work without his lord's privity, let him forfeit his hide (be scourged) or a ransom for it. If a freeman work without his lord's command, let him forfeit his freedom, or sixty shillings. Let a priest be liable in double punishment." To a similar effect were the "dooms," A. D. 696, of Wihtred, King of the Kentish, and also the laws A. D. 878, enacted by the convention between Ædward the

Elder and Guthrun the Dane. These latter, however, went further and ordained that goods set for sale on Sunday should be forfeited. Athelstane likewise, A. D. 925, forbade "buying and selling on the Lord's day." Edgar the Peaceful, A. D. 958, forbade, further, "heathenish songs and diabolical sports," whatever these were, and also markets and county courts. He also fixed the beginning of Sunday at three o'clock Saturday afternoon, to last "till Monday morning light." This extension of Sunday did not last very long. Aethelred (1009) added "hunting bouts" to the prohibited sports, and renewed the interdict as to "trafficking, county courts and worldly works." King Canute—sturdy man as he was—also put hunting (1017) under the ban. He, however, relaxed the rule as to the courts, and allowed them to sit on Sunday "in case of great necessity." The constitution of Archbishop Islip, 1359, complains bitterly "to our great hearts grief * * * that a detestable, nay damnable perverseness has prevailed as to the observance of Sunday"—that though it is provided by sanction of law and canon "that no markets, negotiations or courts be held on that day, and that people go to church, yet, that men neglect their churches for unlawful meetings, where revels and drunkenness and many other dishonest doings are practiced." Following this comes II Richard (1388), forbidding to servants and laborers on Sunday "the playing at tennis, foot ball, and other games called coytes, dice, casting of the stone, railes and such other importune games," but doubtless, with an eye to the good of the state, ordering that they should have "bows and arrows, and use the same on Sunday." This law was reënacted with additional penalties by Henry IV (1404). The same year a statute was ordained that forbade cordwainers and cobblers from selling shoes, &c., on Sunday. This, however, was repealed in 1523. In 1438, under Henry VI, an act was passed forbading laborers, engaged by the week, to claim wages for work done on Sunday. In 1458, under Henry VI, an act was passed stating that "considering the abominable injuries and offences done to Almighty God and His saints (always aiders and singular assistors in our necessities), because of fairs and markets upon their high and principal feasts," forbade the holding of markets and fairs on Sunday, except the four Sundays in harvest. Edward VI, in his injunctions, without waiting for a parliament, ordered that Sunday "be wholly given to God—in hearing the word of God read and taught, in private and public, prayers, * * * visiting the sick," &c., but allowed men in time of harvest to labor on holy and festival days, and save that thing which God hath sent, and adds, that "scrupulosity to abstain from working upon those days doth grievously offend God." The parliament of Edward VI (1552) confirmed this with but little change. All persons were ordered to keep Sundays "holy days," and to abstain from lawful bodily labor, but it was allowed "to every husbandman, laborer, fisherman, and to all and every other person and persons of whatsoever degree or condition he or she may be, upon the holy days aforesaid, in harvest or at any other times in the year, when necessity shall require, to labor, ride, fish, or work any kind of work at their free will and pleasure." The harvest time referred to was then apparently counted from July 1st to September 24th, and was not restricted to four weeks. Under Queen Mary this act was repealed. Queen Elizabeth, who did not suffer her parliament to meddle much with religious matters, re-enjoined its observance, but the act was not revived by parliament till I James, when the act of Queen Mary was formally repealed and this revived. In 1564, Puritanism, which had been at work on the English mind for many years, took definite form and first assumed its name. It intensified yet further the severity and strictness of conduct on Sunday, and apparently, about this time, the name of Sabbath was for the first time applied generally to the day. Fuller mentions, as an incident which increased this feeling, an accident which happened in 1583 at a bull baiting on Sunday: "The scaffold fell and killed a few people, and injured yet more." This, together with Dr. Bownd's book (1583), pushed yet further the tendency of the age to gloom and severity. Queen Elizabeth added to Edward's injunctions by forbidding inn-holders and all house-keepers, &c., "to sell meat or drink in the time of common prayer." This stringency, then as now, produced some reaction. King James I, in one of his progresses through Lancashire, noticed the extreme strictness with which the magistrates compelled the observance of Sunday and the consequent discontent of the people. Therefore, on May 14, 1614, he issued for the people of Lancashire "The Book of Sports," or "Declaration," that his good people after the end of divine service "should not be disturbed, letted or discouraged from any lawful recreations, such as dancing, either of men or women; archery for men, leaping, vaulting or any such harmless recreations, nor from having of May games, Whitsunales or Morris dances, and setting up of May poles, or other sports therewith used, * * * withal prohibiting all unlawful games to be used on Sundays only, as bear baiting, bull baiting, interludes and at all times in the meaner sort of people by law prohibited, bowling." This king who "never said a foolish thing and never did a wise one," well illustrated this unhappy faculty in this declaration. The preamble deserves to be set out in full. "With our own ears," says the king, "we have heard the complaints of our people that they were barred from all lawful recreation and exercise upon the Sunday's afternoon, after the ending of all divine service, which cannot but produce two evils. The one hindering the conversion of many whom their priests will take occasion thereby to vex, persuading them that no honest mirth or recreation is lawful or tolerable in our religion, which cannot but breed a great discontentment in our people's hearts, especially of such as are peradventure upon the point of turning. The other inconvenience is this, that this prohibition barreth the meaner and commoner sort of people from using such exercises as may make their bodies more able for war, when we or our successors shall have occasion to use them, and in place thereof sets up filthy tipplings and drunkenness, and breeds a number of idle and discontented speeches in their ale houses. For when the common people have leave to exercise, if not upon the Sundays and holy days, seeing they must apply to their labor and win their living in all working days." Instead of extending this privilege to all classes, he expressly refused "this benefit and liberty to known recusants" (so-called Romanists), and to the Puritans. This incensed these beyond measure. The calvinistic Archbishop Abbott forbade the reading of this declaration (as required by it), at Croydon Church. The Lord Mayor of London stopped the king's carriage when passing through London on Sunday. In 1618 King James transmitted orders to the clergy of the whole of England to read the declaration from the pulpit, but so strong was the opposition that he prudently withdrew his command. Puritanism was still in the ascendant, and the "Book of Sports" apparently fell a dead letter. It was not extended by this king beyond Lancashire, and the observance of Sunday, under the influence of the calvanistic archbishop, remained generally as strict as ever. In the first year of Charles I, the parliament which he had hastened to call passed an act for the strict observance of Sunday, which the Puritans, who controlled the parliament, affected to call the Sabbath, and which they sanctified by the most melancholy indolence. With that positive knowledge of God's will which has always characterized the Puritans, they assert dogmatically "that the holy keeping of the Lord's day is a principal part of the true service of God," than which service there is nothing more acceptable to him; and then enact that "there shall be no meetings, assemblies or concourse of people out of their own parishes on the Lord's day * * * for any sports and pastimes whatsoever, nor any bear baiting, bull baiting, interludes, common plays or other unlawful exercises and pastimes, be used by any person or persons within their own parishes." The penalty was a fine of three shillings and four pence, and in default of payment the offender "should sit in the stocks for the space of three hours." The broader and more catholic spirit of Laud, then Bishop of London, apparently modified the strictness with which those laws were enforced. Upon the death of Abbot in 1633 he succeeded to the archbishopric, and with the greater power he thus obtained he secured a greater indulgence to sports and pastimes. By his influence, as it was afterwards charged, though apparently not proved, Charles re-published his father's Book of Sports on October 13, 1633, and extended its provisions to the whole realm. This was sorely distasteful to the Puritan clergy, and they avoided reading the book in the churches as far as they could, or, on reading it, would follow it by the fourth commandment, or by a sermon against it. Many of the clergymen were punished for refusing to obey the injunction. Charles was, however, apparently more firm than his father and the book was not altogether a dead letter. Later it was, by order of the Long Parliament, burnt by the common hangman. In the third year of Charles (to go back a little) we find another law of parliament (1627) which enacts that no carriers with any horse, nor wagonmen with any wagon, nor cartmen with any cart, nor wainmen with any wains, nor drover with any cattle * * * by themselves or any other, shall * * * travel on Sunday, nor shall any butcher, by himself, or through any person "kill or sell any victual," on the said day. This brings us to the act which, with that of Charles I just cited, is of most interest and importance to us Americans, *i. e.* the act of 1676. It was of force at the Revolution, and gave more or less color to the laws of the colonies and of the states which succeeded them. For "the better observation and keeping holy the Lord's day, commonly called Sunday," it enacts:

1. That previous laws in force concerning the observation of the Lord's day, and reparing to church therein, be carefully put in execution.

2. That all persons shall apply themselves to such observation by exercising themselves thereon in the duties of piety and true religion, publicly and privately.

3. That no tradesman, artificer, workman, laborer or other person whatsoever "shall do any worldly labor, business or work of their ordinary callings," on that day (works of necessity and charity only excepted)." Children under fourteen years of age were excepted from the operation of this section.

4. That no person shall publicly cry, show forth or expose for sale, any wares, merchandise, fruit, herbs, goods or chattels whatsoever, upon pain of forfeiture of the goods.

5. That no drover, horse courser, wagoner, butcher, higgler, or their servants, shall travel or come to his or their inn or lodging.

6. That no person shall "use, employ or travel * * * with any boat, wherry, lighter, or barge, except on some extraordinary occasion, to be allowed by some magistrate.

7. If any person travelling on Sunday shall be robbed, the Hundred was relieved from the responsibility therefor, but must still make pursuit of the robber.

8. It made void the services of all writs and other legal process on Sunday, except in cases of treason, felony and breach of the peace.

9. That this act should not apply to the prohibiting of dressing of meats in families, or dressing or selling of meats in inns, cook-shops, or victualing houses, for such as other-

wise cannot be provided, "nor to the crying and selling of milk before nine in the morning and after four in the afternoon."

This ends my review of the English statutes on this subject. The later acts do not concern this country. Doubtless I have omitted some that I should have noticed. Still the above gives, I hope, the most material regulations for the observance of Sunday at that time. First, ordinary work is forbidden. Then follows the selling of goods. Then the joyous and rollicking festivities of fairs and markets. Then comes games and sports, and thus gradually Sunday is filled with unhappy associations to many. That bull baiting, bear baiting and such like cruel sports should have been interdicted on the day of rest—the day of peace—seems natural to us, but it will be difficult to assign any religious reason for the prohibition of quoits, foot-ball, &c., while the use of bows and arrows was encouraged. The reason implied in the Book of Sports was doubtless the true one. The English archer made the English infantry of that day peculiarly formidable. The peasants supplied the archers. Cut off from all other amusements on their day of leisure, they were almost compelled to become proficient in archery, and to form a corps of skilled reserves, from which the army could always be recruited. These laws of England, however, did not suit many of the Puritans of that day. They were too moderate for the followers of Dr. Bownd, and these preferred to exchange their old homes for a wild and unknown land, rather than not to have their own laws, and to follow religion according to their own views. These men were too much in earnest in their convictions to brook any half way observance of Sunday, and their influence in this matter is felt among us yet.

We will now turn our attention to the laws of our own state. When the frame of government for Pennsylvania was adopted by Penn, 25th April, 1682, and certain laws were agreed upon by the Governor and freemen of the province, on the 5th May, 1682, it was enacted, *inter alia,* "That according to the good example of the primitive Christians, and for the ease of creation, every first day of the week, called the Lord's day, people shall abstain from the common daily labor, that they may the better dispose themselves to worship God according to their understandings." In the "Great Law" of the province of Pennsylvania and territories thereto belonging, passed at an assembly held at "Chester, *alias* Upland," December 7, 1682, it was again enacted, "To the end that looseness, irreligion and atheism, may not creep in under pretense of conscience in this province, that according to the example of the primitive Christians, and for the ease of creation, every first day of the week, called the Lord's day, people shall abstain from their usual and common toil and labor. That whether masters, parents, children or servants, they may the better dispose themselves to read the scriptures of truth at home or frequent such meetings of religious worship abroad as may best suit their respective persuasions." This was, with some other laws enacted at the same time, declared "a fundamental law," and it was also declared that the same "should not be altered, diminished or repealed in whole or in part without the consent of the Governor, his heirs and assigns and six parts of seven of the freemen of the province or territories thereof in Provincial Council and Assembly met." This and all other laws previously in force were, from their dislike to William Penn, it is said, abrogated by William and Mary, King and Queen of England, in 1693, but this was reënacted by the new provincial authorities the same year and continued in force till the year 1700, when it was again enacted, after the government of the province, which had fallen into great confusion and disorder during the absence of Penn in England, was again reorganized. (See Bioren's Laws, Vol. I, p. 1.) This continued until a new act was passed by the legislature in 1705, which appears to have superseded all previous legislation on this subject, and the fourth, fifth and sixth sections of which are still in force. The first section of this act, which was superseded by the act of 25th April, 1786, and that act by the act of 1794, was as follows:

"An act to restrain people from labor on the first day of the week, to the end that all people in this province may, with greater freedom, devote themselves to religious and pious exercises. Be it enacted by John Evans, Esq., by the Queen's Approbation Lieutenant Governor, under William Penn, Esq., Absolute Proprietary Governor in Chief of the province of Pennsylvania and territories, by and with the advice and consent of the freemen of said province in General Assembly met. That according to the example of the primitive Christians, and for the ease of creation, every first day of the week, commonly called Sunday, all the people shall abstain from toil and labor, that whether masters, parents, children, servants or others, they may the better dispose themselves to read and hear the holy scriptures of truth at home and frequent such meetings of religious worship abroad as may best suit their respective persuasions, and that no tradesman, artificer, workman, laborer or any other person whatsoever, shall do or exercise any worldly business or work of their ordinary callings on the first day of the week, or any part thereof (works of necessity and charity only excepted), upon pain that every person so offending shall, for every offense, forfeit the sum of twenty shillings: *Provided always*, That nothing in this act contained shall extend to prohibit the dressing of victuals in families, cook-shops and victualling houses." In 1794 an act which is now the law of the Commonwealth was passed, superseding and repealing all previous laws, in the terms following:

"An Act for the prevention of vice, immorality and of unlawful gaming, and to restrain disorderly sports and dissipation."

"SECTION I. If any person shall do or perform any worldly employment or business whatever, on the Lord's day, commonly called Sunday (works of charity and necessity only excepted), or shall use or practice any unlawful game, shooting, sport or diversion whatever, on the same day, and be convicted thereof, every such person so offending shall forfeit and pay four dollars, to be levied by distress; or in case he or she shall refuse or neglect to pay said sum, or goods or chattels cannot be found, whereof to levy the same by distress, he or she shall suffer six days' imprisonment in the house of correction of the proper county: *Provided*, That nothing herein contained shall be construed to prohibit the dressing of victuals in private families, bakehouses, inns or other houses of entertainment for the use of sojourners, travellers or strangers, or to hinder watermen from landing their passengers, or ferrymen from carrying over the water travellers, or persons moving with their families on the Lord's day, commonly called Sunday, nor to the delivery of milk, or the necessaries of life, before nine o'clock in the forenoon, nor after five o'clock in the afternoon of the same day."

Judge Duncan, in the case of Updegraph *v*. The Commonwealth, 11 S. &. R. 394, states that "Christianity, general Christianity, is and always has been a part of the common law of Pennsylvania; Christianity without the spiritual artillery of European countries—for this Christianity was one of the considerations of the royal charter and the very basis of its great founder, William Penn—not Christianity with an established church, and tithes, and spiritual courts; not Christianity founded on any particular religious tenets, but Christianity with liberty of conscience to all men. William Penn and Lord Baltimore were the first legislators," the first a Friend, and the latter a Roman Catholic, "who passed laws in favor of liberty of conscience, for before that period the principles of liberty of conscience appeared in the laws of no people, the axiom of no government, the institutes of no society, and scarcely in the temper of any man. Even the reformers were as furious against contumacious errors as they were loud in asserting the liberty of conscience. And to the wilds of America, peopled by a stock cut off by persecution from a Christian society, does Christianity owe true freedom of religious opinion and religious worship." The case was an indictment for blasphemy founded on an Act of Assembly passed in 1700, which enacts that "whosoever shall wilfully, premeditatedly and despitefully blaspheme and speak loosely and profanely of Almighty God, Christ Jesus, the Holy Spirit, or the Scriptures of Truth, and is legally convicted thereof, shall forfeit and pay the sum of ten pounds." It was decided in September, 1824, and the judges of the Supreme Court were Tilghman, Chief Justice, and Gibson and Duncan justices.

The Supreme Court in 1853 was composed of Black, Chief Justice, and Lewis, Lowrie, Woodward and Knox, justices. In the court of that year was the case of Johnson v. The Commonwealth, 10 Harris, 102. It was there held that "driving an omnibus as a public conveyance daily, and every day, is worldly employment, and not a work of charity or necessity within the meaning of the Act of 1794, and therefore not lawful on Sunday. Chief Justice Black and Justice Lewis dissented. Judge Woodward, in delivering the judgment of the court, said: "These statutes were not designed to compel men to go to church or to worship God in any manner inconsistent with personal preferences, but to compel a cessation of those employments which are calculated to interfere with the rights of those who choose to assemble for public worship. The day was set apart for a purpose and the penal enactments guard it, but they leave every man free to use it for that purpose or not. If he wish to use it for the purpose designed, the law protects him from the annoyance of others—if he do not, it restrains him from annoying those who do so use it. Thus the law, without oppressing anybody, becomes auxiliary to the rights of conscience. And there are other rights intimately associated with the rights of conscience which are worth preserving. The right to rear a family with a becoming regard to the institutions of Christianity, and without compelling them to witness, hourly, infractions of one of its fundamental laws; the right to enjoy the peace and good order of society and the increased securities of life and property which result from a decent observance of Sunday; the right of the poor to rest from labor without diminution of wages or loss of employment; the right of beasts of burthen to repose one-seventh of their time from their unrequited toil ; these are real and substantial interests which the legislature sought to secure by this enactment, and when has legislation arrived at higher objects?" The Supreme Court in 1859 was composed of Lowrie, Chief Justice, and Woodward, Thompson, Strong and Read, justices. In the court of that year was the case of The Commonwealth v. Nesbit, 10 Casey, 398. It was there held that "it is not a violation of the Act of April 22, 1794, for a hired domestic servant to drive his employer's family to church on the Lord's day in the employer's private conveyance. Chief Justice Lowrie, in delivering the opinion of the court, said : "Some worldly employments are expressly allowed, such as removing with one's family, delivery of milk and necessaries of life, and the business of ferrymen and innkeepers; and of course, these may be performed by a principal or by his servants, and by all the ordinary means adopted for these purposes, and which are not themselves forbidden. And all worldly employments are allowed which, in their nature, consists of acts of necessity or charity, or if they become so for the time being by reason of famine, flood, fire, pestilence, or other disaster. In such cases necessity and charity demands the work, and with it all the ordinary means of doing it. The whole purpose of some employments is to do works of necessity or charity. The business of a physician cannot be stopped on Sunday because it is a work of necessity. He must travel in performing it, and he is therefore entitled to use all the ordinary means of such travel, and this includes, of course, the labor of his servants in attending to his horse and carriage, and in driving if he thinks it needful. The law does not inquire whether he might have done such work himself. It is not the driving, but the principal work that is needful; the driving follows merely as ordinary means. The business of the apothecary is necessary, so far as it is connected with human sickness, and a man may attend to it by his servants, though that means may not be necessary. Hospitals in great variety are necessary, and no one doubts that all the domestic attendants of these institutions may lawfully pursue their usual avocations therein, because they are the ordinary means of a legitimate purpose. That people may enjoy religious worship and instruction, the functions of the preacher, the religious teacher, the sexton, the organist and the singers are not forbidden, even though these persons engage in these employments as a means of livelihood. Hence, the ordinary means of attending public worship are not forbidden when used purely for this purpose. In this view of the case it is the rightness and the exigencies of the purpose that justify the ordinary means of effectuating it. Conducting and attending religious worship are among the very purposes for which the law protects the day, and therefore all the means which common usage shows to be reasonably necessary for these purposes are not forbidden. But no one ought to expect sharp definitions of legal duty on such a subject. Modes of living, of business, of travel and other human customs are so continually changing that definitions involving them can never be universally, but only generally, adequate. All that we can expect is truth and accuracy to a general intent. Even law, as a definition of human duty, is subject to this defect. Yet, with very few exceptions, it is true that no one who sincerely respects the customs of society and strives to maintain them in his social life, can fail to understand the law in all its main features, and to live in conformity with it. It is only in peculiar and exceptional cases that any difficulties can arise, and even these are made easy of solution by a sincere disposition to conform to the order of society. Necessity itself is totally incapable of any sharp definition. What is a mere luxury or perhaps entirely useless or burdensome to a savage, may be a matter of necessity to a civilized man. What may be a mere luxury or pleasure to a poor man, may be a necessity when he has grown rich. Necessity, therefore, can itself be only approximately defined. The law regards that as necessary which the common sense of the country, in its ordinary modes of doing its business, regards as necessary. By this test the business of keeping a livery stable for the care of people's horses is a necessary employment in large towns, and of course this requires some work and attention on Sundays, and this may be performed to the extent of the necessity by the ordinary means belonging to the business. By this test, also, iron and glass are necessaries of life and they cannot be obtained without some work being done on Sundays, if the business is to be performed according to the ordinary skill and science of the country. The law never inquires whether iron and glass generally, or in such large quantities, are really necessary in the strictest sense of the word, or whether it is not possible to improve the art so that Sunday may not need to be violated. This is not the province of law but of individual enterprise and science. Law, therefore, does not condemn those employments which society regards as necessary, even when they encroach on the Sabbath, if, according to the ordinary skill of the business, it is necessary to do so. And then the business being recognized as necessary, it may be performed by means of the services of others and by all the ordinary means of the business, so far as it is necessary. But let us consider the statutory definition of what is forbidden. It is 'any *worldly* employment or business whatsoever.' What does this word 'worldly' mean? Its correlatives help us to its meaning. Very evidently worldly is contrasted with religions, and the worldly employments are prohibited for the sake of the religious ones. Of course, therefore, no religious employments are forbidden. Hence, funerals, as religious rites, are allowed on Sunday, and all the functions of undertakers, grave diggers, hearse and carriage drivers, and others, though such persons use such employments as a means of livelihood. Hence, also, while purely civil contracts are forbidden on Sunday, marriage is not so, because it is not purely civil, but also a religious contract. But the words domestic, household, family, are also correlatives of the word worldly. If they are so in this law, then worldly employments being alone forbidden, of course these contraries are not. An obstacle to this view is, that cooking victuals in families is excepted as though the general prohibition of worldly employments included it. Yet this exception is possibly expressed by way of precaution to prevent a supposed but perhaps misinterpreted Jewish law from being misapplied to us as though repeated in our law. Exodus, 16: 23 and 35: 3. Or possibly the purpose of the proviso was to save from the prohibition certain worldly employments, such as cooking victuals in bake houses, boarding houses and inns, and delivery of milk, and cooking in families was also named merely to prevent a prohibition of it from being implied from the proviso, though not included in the general prohibition. If this is a redundancy it is not the only one. Cooking victuals in bakehouses and inns is specially allowed, and yet it is understood to be included under the term 'works of necessity.' And if 'worldly employment' is to be taken in its largest sense it includes hunting, shooting and sporting, and yet these are specially forbidden. We think that these terms were not intended to include such household or family work as pertains directly to the proper duties, necessities and comforts of the day, and this work may be done by any member of the family, including domestics. The most convincing proof that this is the true interpetation of the law is, that it has always been so understood. It has never been regarded as applying to the proper internal economy of the family. It does not except the ordinary employments of making fires and beds, cleaning up chambers and fire places, washing dishes, feeding cattle and harnessing horses for going to church, because these were never regarded as the worldly business of the family, and therefore not forbidden to the head of the family or to the domestics. It is probable, however, that the most of these occupations may have been regarded as works of necessity, or as means of performing such work. These domestic employments, being necessary for every day are not worldly employments in the sense of the law, may be exercised in the ordinary modes and with the ordinary freedom of the family without any violation of the law."

The Supreme Court in 1867 was composed of Woodward, Chief Justice, and Thompson, Strong, Read and Agnew, justices. In the court of that year was the case of Sparhawk *v.* Union Passenger Railway Company, 54 Pennsylvania State Reports, 401, where it was held that "running passenger cars on Sunday is a violation of the Act of 1794, and is within its penalties," but that "a party cannot vindicate others' rights by process in his own name nor employ civil process to punish wrongs to the public." Judge

Thompson delivered the opinion of the court which was concurred in by the Chief Justice, and Read, justice. Judge Strong and Agnew dissented. Judge Read, one of the most scholarly men of his day, said in his concurring opinion:

"Christianity is a part of the laws of England, says Blackstone, and Lord Chief Baron Kelly, in the late case of Cowen *v.* Milbourn, Law Rep. 2 Ex. 234, uses similar language: 'There is abundant authority for saying that Christianity is part and parcel of the law of the land.' It is clear, therefore, that, as our common law is derived from England, we must look to that country for information as to what our common law on this subject was and is. England, at least for the last eight hundred years, has always had an established church, with the single exception of the time of the Commonwealth. From William the Conqueror to Henry the VIII it was the Roman Catholic, and from his death to the present time, with the exception of the reign of Queen Mary, it has been the Church of England. Of course this part of the common law has been affected and controlled and formed by the practices and usages of the church, established by law, and not by those of any other sect or denomination of Christians. England has an established church, and Scotland has also another, and neither have any control over the other. Our common law, however, is derived from England, and therefore it is only to England we are to look for it, and not to any other country. The first day of the week, the Lord's day, commonly called Sunday, is a day for worship and rest as regulated by the civil authority. It is *dies non juridicus* in England, but in other respects it is the subject of positive regulation by the legislative authority. I am aware that some religious persons of some religious sects think the sanctity of Sunday, as a day of entire rest, is prescribed to all nations, and particularly to all Christians, by the fourth commandment in the Decalogue, but an attentive perusal of the 20th,

31st and 35th chapters of Exodus, and of the 5th chapter of Deuteronomy, will show that this commandment was specially limited to the Jewish nation alone. The words spoken were, 'I am the Lord thy God, which have brought thee out of the land of Egypt, out of the house of bondage,' and the verses succeeding the Decalogue, and the 21st chapter which commences, 'Now these are the judgments which thou shalt set before them,' show clearly that the commandments and judgments were addressed to the Israelites alone, and so in the 24th chapter, where the people take the covenant and said, 'all that the Lord hath said, will we do, and be obedient.' So in the 12th to the 17th verses of the 31st chapter, 'speak thou also unto the children of Israel, saying, verily my Sabbaths ye shall keep, for it is a sign between me and you throughout your generations.' 'Every one that defileth it shall surely be put to death ; for whosoever doeth any work therein, that soul shall be cut off from among his people.' 'Wherefore, the children of Israel shall keep the Sabbath, to observe the Sabbath throughout their generations for a perpetual covenant.' 'It is a sign between me and the children of Israel forever.' In the 5th chapter of Deuteronomy, 'Moses called all Israel and said unto them, hear, O Israel, the statutes and judgments which I speak in your ears this day, that ye may learn them, and keep, and do them. The Lord our God made a covenant with us in Horeb. The Lord made not this covenant with our fathers, but with us, even us, who are all of us here alive this day.' Then follows the Decalogue, but the reason assigned for the fourth commandment is in the 15th verse in these words, 'And remember that thou wast a servant in the land of Egypt, and that the Lord thy God brought thee out thence through a mighty hand, and by a stretched-out arm : therefore the Lord thy God commanded thee to keep the Sabbath day.' In the 22d verse Moses says, 'These words (the ten commandments) the Lord spake unto all your assembly in the mount, out of the midst of the fire, of the cloud and of the thick darkness, with a great voice; and he added no more.' This recapitulation of Scripture makes it clear that the fourth commandment, which is a positive statute imposed upon the Israelites alone, as a people separated from all other nations by the Almighty for special and wise purposes, was not intended either for the Gentiles or for those living under a later dispensation. Like circumcision, it was a sign between Him and them only. It was a part of the ceremonial law, like sacrifices, and not binding at any time on any nation except the Jews. It is evident that no great nation of modern times, living under the Christian dispensation, could submit to an observance of a day of entire rest under the penalty of death for any breach of it; for the command of the Almighty inflicted this penalty on the offender. The whole Jewish constitution was framed for a small and partially barbarous nation, whose tendency was to idolatry, and upon whom were imposed burdens which could only be borne by those who considered themselves as specially selected by the Godhead. It was not a nation who could spread their doctrines or convert other nations, and their mission ceased with the birth of our Saviour. The Old Testament contains moral revealed law, ceremonial and judicial laws—the two last being either typical, or intended especially or only for the Jewish people under the old dispensation, were terminated by fulfillment or abrogation on the coming of Christ, and the completion of the Christian dispensation. This was the view of the Apostle Paul, when he says in his Epistle to the Colossians, 'Blotting out the handwriting of ordinances that was against us, which was contrary to us, and took it out of the way, nailing it to his cross; and having spoiled principalities and powers, he made a show of them openly, triumphing over them in it. Let no man therefore judge you in meat, or in drink, or in respect of an holy day, or of the new moon, or of the Sabbath days; which are a shadow of things to come: but the body is of Christ.' Col. ii: 14, 15. So in his Epistle to the Galations: 'But now, after that ye have known God, or rather are known of God, how turn ye again to the weak and beggarly elements, whereunto ye desire again to be in bondage? Ye observe days, and months, and times, and years. I am afraid of you, lest I have bestowed upon you labor in vain.' Gal. iv: 9, 10. 'Stand fast, therefore, in the liberty wherewith Christ hath made us free, and be not entangled again with the yoke of bondage.' Gal. v: 1. So in his Epistle to the Romans, 14th chap., 5th verse, 'One man esteemeth one day above another; another esteemeth every day alike. Let every man be fully persuaded in his own mind.' 'He that regardeth the day regardeth it unto the Lord; and he that regardeth not the day, to the Lord he doth not regard it;' and in the preceding chapter, 9th verse, the Apostle says: 'For this, thou shalt not commit adultery; thou shalt not kill; thou shalt not steal; thou shalt not bear false witness; thou shalt not covet; and if there be any other commandment, it is briefly comprehended in this saying, namely, thou shalt love thy neighbor as thyself.' It is evident from these texts that the Apostle did not regard the fourth commandment as a part of the moral revealed law, but as a ceremonial or judicial law which was terminated by the coming of our Saviour and the completion of the Christian dispensation. It was part and parcel of the old dispensation fitted only for a small and peculiar nation, and necessarily perished with it, the whole being supplied by the Christian dispensation embracing in its outstretched arms, not a single people, but all the nations of the earth, and announcing principles of the purest morality exemplified in the life and teachings of the divine author of our religion. The fourth commandment was a positive statute, fixing the seventh day of the week as a day of rest, and is the day observed by the Jews; and of course the first day of the week cannot be the Sabbath day of the Decalogue. The Sunday of the Christian world is therefore not the Jewish Sabbath of the fourth commandment, and such was the declared opinion of Luther, Calvin, and all the early reformers. Luther said: 'As for the Sabbath or Sunday there is no necessity for its observance; and if we do so the reason ought to be not because Moses commanded it, but because nature likewise teaches us to give from time to time a day of rest, in order that man and beast may recruit their strength, and that we may go and hear the word preached.' 'The Gospel regardeth neither Sabbath nor holidays, because they endured but for a time and were ordained for the sake of preaching, to the end God's word might be tended and taught.' 'Keep the Sabbath holy for its use both to body and soul; but if anywhere the day is made holy for the mere day's sake—if anywhere one sets up its observance upon a *Jewish* foundation, then I order you to work on it, to ride on it, to dance on it, to feast on it, to do anything that shall remove this encroachment on the Christian spirit and liberty.' Calvin says in his exposition of the fourth commandment, 'The Fathers frequently called it a *shadowy commandment*, because it contains the external observance of the day, which was abolished with the rest of the figures at the advent of Christ.' 'But all that it (the Sabbath) contained of a ceremonial nature was without doubt abolished by the advent of the Lord Christ.' 'Though the Sabbath is abrogated, yet still it is customary among us to assemble on stated days for hearing the word, for breaking the mystical bread, and for public prayers, and also to allow servants and laborers remission from their labor.' 'They complain that Christians are tinctured with Judaism, because they retain any observance of days. But I reply, the Lord's day is not observed by us upon the principle of Judaism; because, in this respect, the difference between us and the Jews is very great, for we celebrate it, not with scrupulous rigor as a ceremony which we conceive to be a figure of some spiritual mystery, but only use it as a remedy necessary to the preservation of order in the Church.' 'They' (Luther and Calvin), says Rev. Dr. Rice, 'have observed the form rather as a matter of necessity or expediency, than as divinely commanded.' Calvin encouraged the burghers of Geneva by his own presence and example at their public recreations, as bowling and shooting, upon the Lord's day after their devotions at church were ended. Barclay, in his Apology, says: 'We not seeing any ground in Scripture for it, cannot be so superstitious as to believe that either the Jewish Sabbath now continues, or that the first day of the week is the antitype thereof, or the true Christian Sabbath; which, with Calvin, we believe to have a more spiritual sense; and therefore, we know no moral obligation by the fourth command or elsewhere, to keep the first day of the week more than any other, or any holiness in it. But, 1st, forasmuch as it is necessary that there be sometime set apart for the servants to meet together to wait upon God, and that 2dly, it is fit at sometimes they be freed from their *outward* affairs, and that 3dly, reason and equity doth allow that servants and beasts have some time allowed them to be eased from their constant labor, and that 4thly, it appears that the Apostles and primitive Christians did use the first day of the week for these purposes, we find ourselves sufficiently moved for these causes to do so also, without superstitiously straining the Scripture for another reason, which is, that is not to be there found, many Protestants—yea, Calvin himself upon the fourth command hath abundantly evinced.' Melancthon, Beza, Bucer, Zuinglius, Cranmer, Milton and Knox were of the same opinion, and Jeremy Taylor says: 'The effect of which consideration is this: that the Lord's day did not succeed in the place of the Sabbath; but the Sabbath was wholly abrogated and the Lord's day was merely of *ecclesiastical institution.*' Paley, Arnold of Rugby, Archbishop Whately and our great lawgiver hold the same language. Penn says: 'To call any day of the week a *Christian Sabbath* is not *Christian* but *Jewish;* give us one Scripture for it; I will give two against it.' Bishop White, the chaplain to congress during the revolution, and the senior bishop of the Protestant Episcopal Church in the United States of America, in his lectures on the Catechism, p. 64, speaking of the fourth commandment, says: 'In regard to its duration it appears evident that as far as regarded the authority of the injunction to the Israelites, and unless some new obligation can be shown the institution ceased even in relation to Jewish converts to Christianity at the destruction of their religious polity; *and that it never extended to the Gentile Christians.* Of this there shall be given but one proof; it being decisive to the point. It is in the second chapter of the Epistle to the Colossians: 'Let no man, therefore, judge you in meat, or in drink, or in respect of an holy day, or of the new moon, or of the Sabbath days.' Here the Sabbath is considered as falling with the whole body of the ritual law of Moses, and this may show the reason on which our church avoids the calling of her day of public worship— 'The Sabbath.' It is never so called in the New Testament.' And in the primitive church the term 'Sabbatizing' carried with it the reproach of a leaning to the abrogated observances of the law.' The late Rev. Dr. James W. Alexander, a very distinguished divine of the Presbyterian Church, writing from New York, says: 'The question of riding in our street cars on Sunday is agitating our community. I have not been able to decide it. THE POOR GO IN CARS, THE RICH IN COACHES. The number of horses and men is less than if there were no cars. It is a query whether as many cars as would be demanded by those (among half a million), who have lawful occasion to journey. If so, the whole question would be reduced to one of individual vocation to this amount of locomotion. The whole matter of the Christian Sabbath is a little perplexed to my mind. 1st. All that our Lord says on it is *prima facie* on the side of relaxation. 2d. The Apostles who enforce, and, as it were, reënact every other commandment of the ten, never advert to this. 3d. Even to Gentile converts they lay no stress on this, which might be expected to come first among externals. 4th. According to the letter, Paul teaches the Colossians (xi: 16), not to be scrupulous about Sabbaths. I am not, therefore, surprised, Calvin had doubts on the subject. I must wait for more light.' To the young man whom he directed to keep the commandments, if he would enter into eternal life, and who asked him, 'Which?' 'Jesus said, thou shalt do no murder; thou shalt not commit adultery; thou shalt not steal; thou shalt not bear false witness; honor thy father and thy mother, and thou shalt love thy neighbor as thyself,' is a strong corroboration of the second reason above given by Dr. Alexander. The Sabbath of the fourth commandment being abrogated and abolished, our Saviour did not command the observance of Sunday, nor is it alleged that there is any express direction to observe it by any of the Apostles to be found in the New Testament. That Sunday (*dies solis*) grew up by usage among the primitive Christians as a stated day of prayer, and was recognized as such in the time of Justin Martyr, is certain. But it was clearly not a Sabbath in the Jewish sense, for the division into weeks was not recognized in the Roman world until the third and fourth centuries, and all Christians who were slaves could not have obliged their heathen masters to give them one day in seven, for an entire rest from all labor. So, from Pliny's letter to the Emperor Trajan, it would appear, the primitive Christians met before it was light for worship and prayer, which was obviously adopted that it might not interrupt the labors or occupations of the day, a large portion of these early disciples belonging to the servile and laboring classes. When Christianity became the religion of the emperor, and of course of the state, we find the division into weeks used, and the days called by the planetary names, as *dies solis* (day of the sun), *dies lunæ* (day of the moon), &c. The act for keeping holidays and fast days of the 5th and 6th Edward the 6th, chap. 3 (1552), is framed upon the same principle as the edict of Constantine, and speaking of the days appointed for the worship of God, which are called Holy Days, says this, 'not for the matter and nature, either of the time or day;' 'for so all days and times considered are God's creatures, and all of like holiness. Neither is it to be thought that there is any certain time or definite number of days prescribed in holy scripture, but that the appointment, both of the time and also the number of days is left by the authority of God's word to the liberty of Christ's Church, to be determined and assigned, orderly in every country, by *the discretion of the rulers and ministers thereof*, as they shall judge most expedient to the true setting forth of God's glory and the edification of their people.' Then follow the holy days to be kept, 'all Sundays in the year.' These are festivals. In Swann *v*. Broome, 3 Burr. 1595, it was decided that Sunday was *dies non juridicus*, and Lord Mansfield says: 'Anciently the courts of justice did sit on Sunday. The fact of this, and the reasons of it, appear in Sir Henry Spellman's original of the terms.' It appears, by what he says, that the ancient Christians practised this. In his chapter of law days among the first Christians, using all days alike, he says, 'the Christians at first used all days alike for hearing of causes, not sparing (as it seemeth) the Sunday itself.' They had two reasons for it. One was in opposition to the heathens, who were superstitious about the observation of days and times, conceiving some to be ominous and unlucky, and others to be lucky; and therefore the

Christians laid aside all observance of days; a second reason they also had, which was by keeping their own courts *always open*, to prevent Christian suitors from resorting to the heathen courts. In Mackalley's Case, 9 Co., it was '*Resolved*, That no judicial act ought to be done on that day; but ministerial acts may be lawfully executed on the Sunday.' These cases are distinctly affirmed in Huidekoper *v.* Cotton, 3 Watts, 59; Kepner *v.* Keefer, 6 Id. 231; Fox *v.* Mensch, 3 W. & S. 444. It is clear, therefore, that in England, Sunday, or the Lord's day, was considered an ecclesiastical institution, and the only common law restraint imposed upon it, as an observance of the day, was that no judicial proceedings should be had on Sunday, and that courts should not sit on that day. In early times Parliament sat on Sunday; for in the reign of Edward the First, in 1278 and 1305, three statutes were made on Sunday, and Froude, in his first vol. of the History of Henry the Eighth, p. 67, speaking of the English archery, says: 'Every hamlet had its pair of butts, and on Sundays and holidays all able bodied men were required to appear in the field, to employ their leisure hours 'as valyant Englishmen ought to do,' utterly leaving the play at the bowls, quoits, dice, kails and other unthrifty games. On the same days the tilt-yard, at the hall or castle, was thrown open, and the young men of rank amused themselves with similar exercises.' By the Act of 3 and 4 William, 4 ch. 31, reciting that the profanation of the Lord's day is greatly increased by certain meetings, which are usually or occasionally held on that day, it enacts that all such meetings of corporations, vestries and public companies, and every other meeting of a public and secular nature required to be held on any Lord's day, shall be held on the preceding Saturday or succeeding Monday. It is therefore evident that the Lord's day was considered like any other day, to be subject to regulation by the civil authority alone, who could, if it were deemed expedient and necessary, authorize the courts to sit on Sunday, notwithstanding the common law prohibition. By the Act of the 29 Charles 2, ch. 7, for the better observance of the Lord's day, commonly called Sunday, no tradesman, artificer, workman, laborer or other person whatsoever, shall do or exercise any worldly labor or work of their ordinary callings, upon the Lord's day or any part thereof (works of necessity and charity only excepted), 'under a penalty of five shillings.' Under this statute, it has been held, a sale of a horse was not void, such sale not being made in the ordinary calling of the plaintiff or his agent, so a contract of hiring made on a Sunday between a farmer and a laborer for a year is valid, and the enlistment of a soldier by a recruiting officer is not within the statute. The words 'other person or persons' do not include the owner or driver of a stage coach, and therefore, their contracts to carry passengers on a Sunday are binding; so an attorney, entering into an agreement on Sunday for the settlement of his client's affairs, and thereby rendering himself personally liable, is not thereby exercising his usual calling; and the penalty can only be incurred once on the same day. So a farmer engaged in haymaking on Sunday is not within the statute; nor are railways. 'The statutes clearly do not apply to railway companies, so as to render it illegal for them to run trains for the conveyance of goods or passengers on a Sunday.' Chitty on Carriers, 117. Such was the law of England at the foundation of the Province of Pennsylvania by William Penn, for although railways were not in existence, stage coaches were, in 1658, in Cromwell's time. Penn's views on the subject of Sunday are to be found in his works and those of Barclay, and were the views of the Society of Friends, who were the early colonists. In the laws agreed upon in England expression is given to them in the 36th law: 'That according to the good example of the primitive Christians, and for the ease of the creation, every first day of the week, called the Lord's day, people shall abstain from their common daily labor, that they may the better dispose themselves to worship God according to their understandings.' With all Penn's liberality, we find by Janney's life of him, he was strictly orthodox in his own belief. p. 575. It is certain also that he agreed with Luther and Calvin, and the statute of Edward 6th, as to the institution of the Lord's day, and that the mode of observance of it should be prescribed by the civil authority. In 1705 was passed the act to restrain people from labor on the first day of the week, which is copied *verbatim* from the English statute, in the prohibitory part of the first section to which a penalty is attached, and is therefore to be construed in the same way, which would not have brought either stage coaches or railways, if they had been in existence, within the act. This remained the law until the 30th of March, 1779, when an act for the suppression of vice and immorality was passed, by the 2d section of which it was enacted, 'that if any person shall do any kind of work of his or her ordinary calling, or follow or do any worldly employment or business whatsoever on the Lord's day, commonly called Sunday (works of necessity and mercy only excepted),' he should be fined. This act not having been enforced, and the fine, being payable in depreciated currency, having become less than a shilling in specie currency, another act was passed on the 25th September, 1786, forbidding, under a penalty, any person doing or performing any worldly employment or business whatsoever on the Lord's day, commonly called Sunday (works of necessity and charity only excepted); 'Provided, always, that nothing in this act contained, shall be construed to prohibit the dressing of victuals in private families, bake houses or in lodging houses, wine and other houses of entertainment for the use of sojourners, travellers or strangers, or to hinder watermen from landing their passengers, or stage coaches, or stage wagons from carrying travellers (having the consent of a justice of the peace upon extraordinary occasions), on the Lord's day, commonly called Sunday, nor to the delivery of milk or other necessaries of life, before nine o'clock in the forenoon, nor after five of the clock in the afternoon of the same day.' Then came the Act of the 22d of April, 1794, which was passed the year after the yellow fever had devastated our city, and which is the existing law. The first section enacts that, 'if any person shall do or perform any worldly employment or business whatsoever on the Lord's day, commonly called Sunday (works of necessity and charity only excepted), he shall, for every such offence, forfeit and pay four dollars.' It will be observed that the Act of 1682 contained no penalty, which was, however, supplied by the Act of 1700; but the Act of 1705, like the statute of Car. 2, did not apply to stage coaches or to travellers by public conveyances, and this was the wise and liberal law of the province under which grew up the usages mentioned by C. J. Lowrie, in Commonwealth *v.* Nesbit, 10 Casey, 398, and which would be illegal under a strict construction of the Act of 1794. In 1779 and 1786 the language was changed, and this accounts for the exception of stage coaches in the proviso of the last named act. The cardinal error in Johnston *v.* Commonwealth, 10 Harris, 109, in the omnibus case, is in treating Sunday as set apart by divine command, and from the whole decision two judges, two-fifths of the court, dissented in opinions of very great weight and force ; and the error in Commonwealth *v.* Nesbit, 10 Casey, 398, was in assuming that usages, which were considered exceptions, had grown up under laws of a similar character, which we have seen was not the case, instead of treating them as works of necessity, which they clearly are. Judge Bell, in Specht *v.* Commonwealth, 8 Barr, 325, puts the Sunday law on its true basis : 'Its sole mission is to inculcate a temporary weekly cessation from labor, but it adds not to this requirement any religious obligation.' I shall therefore treat the case before us as one within the exceptions of necessity and charity. Before doing so, it will be proper to consider the history of this prohibitory law. With us it binds all persons, whether Israelites or Seventh-day Christians. In Maine, Massachusetts, Connecticut, New York and Ohio, persons who conscientiously believe and keep the seventh day as holy time, may do secular work and labor on Sunday, provided they disturb no other persons; and in Connecticut the prohibition to do any work is limited to that portion of the day between the rising of the sun and the setting of the same. Our very illiberality should make us more desirous to extend the limits of necessity and charity, and not to confine them within narrow boundaries in this age of improvement. After another season of pestilence, the legislature, on the 4th April, 1798, passed an act to prevent the disturbance of religious societies in the city of Philadelphia during the time of divine service, which, after reciting the Act of the 6th February, 1731, relating to religious societies, and stating that they had purchased lots and erected churches, and other houses of religious worship, and that by the constitution of this Commonwealth it is declared 'that all men have a natural and indefeasible right to worship Almighty God according to the dictates of their conscience.' 'And whereas, it would be nugatory to grant the said rights without securing the peaceable and quiet enjoyment of them;' it then enacted that the religious societies aforesaid were each authorized by a suitable person 'to extend and fasten so many chains across the streets, lanes or alleys,' as may be sufficient *to hinder and obstruct* all coaches, coachees, chariots, chaises, wagons and other carriages whatsoever, and all and every person or persons, riding or travelling on horseback, from passing by the said churches or houses of religious worship during the time of divine service therein.' They were only to be extended across the streets on Sundays, nor then until the commencement of divine service within said churches; said chains to be taken down before dusk and immediately after divine service is ended in the same. The iron sockets in which the posts were fixed to which the chains were attached, are still to be seen opposite some of the old churches. In 1816 this act was extended to the incorporated district of the Northern Liberties, and both acts were repealed in 1831, showing that the public were convinced that the passage of these vehicles and horses, neither disturbed the congregations during divine service, nor injured the property, or decreased the value of the churches. In England the railroads are *not compelled* to run on Sundays, but whenever they do, they are obliged to provide a cheap train also, which shall stop at all the usual stations, so as to accommodate poor persons. Some sixteen years ago the directors of the railway between Glasgow and Edinburgh stopped the Sunday train, except the mail car, which they were obliged to run to carry the mail. This road has been lately purchased by the North British Railway Company, who have resumed the Sunday trains, much to the comfort of the people. It is not astonishing that the Scottish clergy, who are all of one denomination, should be very strict in their Sunday observances, when it was thought improper to walk on Sunday afternoon, after divine service, for recreation, and when in some parts of Scotland a clergyman cannot shave himself on Sunday morning, because it is an infraction of the fourth commandment, 'In it thou shalt do no manner of work.' In 1658 the Presbytery of Strathbogie condemned an offender accused of Sabbath breaking for saving the life of a sheep. All other modes of passing from one part of the state to another are extinguished, and travelling by private conveyance no longer exists. If the Sunday prohibition extends to railroads, then no errand of mercy, at any distance from the city, can ever be accomplished on that day. I have had a personal experience of the value of Sunday trains; for on a Sunday I was enabled to take a most distinguished physician, who could not leave the city on any other day, to see a sick sister, at thirty miles distant, leaving after breakfast and returning before dinner. I have therefore no hesitation in saying, that I consider Sunday trains as coming within the exceptions of necessity and charity. The Commonwealth v. Nesbit was decided in the autumn of 1859, eight years ago, and Chief Justice Lowrie said: 'The law regards that as necessary, which the common sense of the country, in its ordinary modes of doing its business, regards as necessary.' There are now four passenger railways in Pittsburg, operating seventeen miles of road, and passing in front of churches of every sect and denomination, and all running on Sunday, and used and patronized by divines, judges, and all the religious persons in the community. They have met with universal approbation, and the Sunday cars have become a matter of absolute necessity in taking persons to and from church, and have conduced greatly to the peace and quiet of the city and suburbs. This is the universal belief, and I know it to be correct, having frequently ridden in them on Sunday. Sunday cars are used in Boston, New York, Albany, Troy and Brooklyn, in Hoboken and Jersey City in New Jersey, Baltimore, Nashville, Cincinnati, Washington, St. Louis and Chicago, and give universal satisfaction. Within the last ten years, 167 miles of passenger railway have been built and worked in this city, which have entirely superseded the omnibuses, which had numbered 400, and have virtually dispensed with all other means of general locomotion in this city. At the time of the passage of the Sunday law, the population of the city of Philadelphia was under 30,000, and we now have within the corporate limits a population nearly double that of the whole state in 1790, when Pittsburg had but 1200 souls, and the county of Erie was not the property of the commonwealth. Some of the vehicles named in the Act of 1798, are now known only by tradition, and an entire and radical change has taken place in the means of locomotion accommodated to a municipality of 130 square miles in area, with 100,000 dwellings, and with streets extending miles in length, and many of them separated by a navigable stream, which increases the difficulty of passing from one part of the city to another. In 1794 we had no waterworks, no iron pipes, no steamboats, no canals, no railroads, no gas, no telegraph, no Atlantic cable, and only one stone turnpike—all of which are matters of indispensable necessity, and coming clearly within the necessity exception of the Sunday law. In 1856 the first passenger railway was chartered. The passenger railways to-day, in the short period of eleven years, traverse nearly every portion of the city, and pass over the Schuylkill by the bridges at Chestnut and Market streets, at Fairmount and Girard avenue. The rails laid are broad, and accommodate all vehicles, whether for pleasure or burden, with a smooth surface, diminishing greatly the noise and the labor of the horses. To an invalid nothing can be more grateful than to escape from the cobblestones, and to ride on the railway track. It has been decided that no person can claim damages from a company whose road passes on a street in front of his property. These passenger railways are therefore legal institutions, and the owners of the tracks laid on the streets subject to a modified user by the public. Workmen and laboring men are enabled by these railways to work a long way from their homes without the fatigue of walking long distances, and the consequent loss of time; men of business, old persons, invalids, women and children, are enabled to ride on their different errands at a small expense. Our city spreads out in every direction, because distances are in fact annihilated by the passenger railways. The stoppage of these railways would utterly derange the whole business of the city, reduce the value of all property, and entirely destroy the present prosperous condition of our metropolis. The railways are therefore an absolute necessity, and are clearly within the exception of the statute. These railways are in operation a very large portion of the twenty-four hours, and in some instances every hour of the twenty-four. Their necessity in cold, wind, rain, hail, sleet and snow, and in the heats of midsummer, all acknowledge. Most of the plaintiffs, if not all, have places of business on streets where passenger cars are passing every few minutes, and no one has complained that they have ever interfered with his addition of items in a bill, in his correspondence with his customers, or the details of his trade or occupation. Clergymen and religious persons have family worship on week days, and meetings for religious worship are held on various days besides Sundays, but I have never heard that the cars disturbed them or interfered with the prayers put up by pious men on every day in the year in their own dwellings, except in the single case of Sunday. People sleep whilst the cars are running, and no one complains of them as a nuisance. The greatest nuisance is the driving up of carriages during the sermon to take home at the close of the service the rich members of the congregation. There are two services a day, occupying two hours in the morning, and two hours in the afternoon, say four hours out of the twenty-four, and to protect these four hours we are asked to enjoin the whole day. When there is no religious worship a church experiences no inconvenience, and its complaint is like that of an owner of an uninhabited dwelling, and entitled to no more consideration. It is certain that a railway car, rolling over a smooth iron rail, occasions no more real noise than a wagon or a carriage driven smartly over a cobblestone pavement. It is to be recollected that this noise of the rolling of the cars is legal, and authorized by Acts of Assembly, and therefore it is *damnum absque injuria,* and it clearly is not such an annoyance 'as materially to interfere with the ordinary comfort of human existence,' and neither of the plaintiffs could obtain *any damages,* much less substantial damages at law, so as to entitle him to an injunction. Crump *v.* Lambert, Law Rep. 3 Eq. 409. As to disturbing persons in private dwellings on Sunday, it is an absurdity, which requires no answer. If, therefore, the churches, or rather the individual pewholders, have no right to complain, what right have these plaintiffs to deny others the right of locomotion, in order to force them to attend church in the very teeth of the constitutional provision, 'that no man can of right be compelled to attend, erect or support any place of worship, or to maintain any ministry against his consent.' Having established the absolute necessity, in the present state of our city, of passenger railways, and the utter impracticability of doing without them, why should there be one day in seven in which that necessity must cease, and not operate? All that ceases on Sunday is common toil or labor, and the intention is to protect the laboring man who earns his bread by the sweat of his brow. Besides worship and prayer, there are hours for healthful and innocent recreation. These are protected by the constitutional provision. We have public squares and a great public park owned by our fellow citizens, and intended for their benefit and that of their wives and children. Clergymen, lawyers, physicians, merchants, and even judges, have six days in the week in which they may enjoy all these and other similar advantages, and which they may do so cheaply by means of the passenger railways. The laboring man, the mechanic, the artisan, has but one day in which he can rest, can dress himself and his family in their comfortable Sunday clothes, attend church, and then take healthful exercise; but, by this injunction, his carriage—*the poor man's carriage, the passenger car*—is taken away, and is not permitted to run for his accommodation. The laboring man and his children are never allowed to see Fairmount Park, a part of his own property. The cars are required on Sunday to carry persons to and from church, and are not these church going people entitled to have them? The necessity for this clearly exists on Sunday, and so it does enable persons to partake of the fresh air in the squares and parks and in the country. But we should not oblige the working man to confine himself to his own narrow, stifling room, and forbid him to enjoy the fresh air of heaven. We have three long months of summer which the laboring man cannot escape. Merchants, manufacturers, lawyers, judges and physicians run away from them, and even clergymen leave their churches, and go to the seashore or to the mountains, to avoid the torrid months of July and August. Shall not the operative have the poor privilege allowed him of a passenger car on Sunday? The same necessity exists on Sunday as on any other day, enhanced by the fact that you are preventing thousands from attending houses of religious worship. I place my opinion, therefore, of the entire legality of running passenger cars on Sunday, on the same footing with the Sunday trains of the steam railroads, as being clearly within the exceptions both of necessity and charity. The mail protects nothing but the mail car on the steam railroads, and many of the trains carry no mail at all. If I conceded the illegality, still it would be clear to me that these plaintiffs have no standing in this court, and no right to ask for any injunction against these defendants. It is a matter for the commonwealth alone, 'and she has her own chosen officers to protect her own rights, and the rights of the whole community are what constitute public rights, or the rights of the commonwealth.' I am deeply impressed with the necessity of a proper observance of Sunday as a day of worship and prayer and of rest from labor; but living under the new dispensation, and not under the old dispensation, I feel no inclination to turn the Lord's day into a *Jewish Sabbath.*"

Thus the law stands in Pennsylvania, and thus in substance it has stood since the establishment of the provincial government of William Penn in 1682. I now close the review of the Sunday laws as they have come down to us. No one can be more conscious how defective this sketch is than the writer. There is nothing new in it, and I know that it is imperfect. I have derived great satisfaction in the study of the subject and hope that it will prove equally interesting to all who read it.

OLD FORGE.

EARLY METHODISM.

OLD FORGE—EARLY METHODISM.

Remarks by George B. Kulp at the dedication of the Stewart Memorial Church, at Old Forge, Pa., April 26, 1892.

"And the captain of the Lord's host said unto Joshua, Loose thy shoe from off thy foot, for the place whereon thou standest is holy."

In the year 1791, in this immediate vicinity, the first Methodist Class, in what is now Lackawanna county, was held. It was also the most northern point in Pennsylvania in which Methodism had been established. James Sutton was the leader, and the Class was held at the house of Captain John Vaughan. Old Forge derived its name from Dr. William Hooker Smith, who, after his return from General Sullivan's expedition, located himself permanently here on the rocky edge of the Lackawanna beside the sycamore and oak where first, in the Lackawanna valley, the sound of the trip-hammer reverberated or mingled with the hoarse babblings of its water. The forge was erected by Dr. Smith and James Sutton, in the spring of 1789, for converting ore into iron. It stood immediately below the falls or rapids in the stream, between two and three miles above its mouth. Hon. Charles Miner says: "My recollections of Pittston and Old Forge are all of the most cheerful character—but to the Forge—the heaps of charcoal and bog ore, half a dozen New Jersey firemen at the furnace. What life, what clatter. And then at the mansion on the hill" (near the old Drake store) "might be seen the owner, Dr. William Hooker Smith, now nearly superannuated, who, in his day, was the great physician of the valley, and if perchance the day was

NOTE.—The Stewart Memorial Church was erected by Mrs. George B. Kulp, Mrs. Charles B. Scott, Mrs. William D. Loomis and Mrs. Lewis C. Hessler, as a Memoriam to their late parents, Mr. and Mrs. John Stewart, of Scranton, Pa.

fine and his family on the parterre, you might see his daughters, unsurpassed in beauty and grace, whose every movement was harmony, that would add a charm to the proudest city mansion." We might say in this connection that Dr. Smith was not, and never became, a Methodist. In his will, written by his own hand, and dated March 19, 1810, he uses the following language: "I recommend my soul to Almighty God that gave it to me, nothing doubting but that I shall be finally happy. My destiny, I believe, was determined unalterably before I had existence. God does not leave any of his works at random subject to chance, but in what place, where or how I shall be happy, I know not." And at the close of his will was the following: "Now, to the Sacred Spring of all mercies and Original Fountain of all goodness to the Infinite and Eternal being whose purpose is unalterable, whose power and dominion is without end, whose compassion fails not; to the High and Lofty One who inhabits eternity and dwells in light be glory, majesty, dominion and power now and for evermore. Amen." The first permanent settlement in the Wyoming Valley was in 1769. In that year or the next Connecticut people settled in Pittston, as this neighborhood was then called. The first saw and grist mills in the Lackawanna Valley were built by the town (Pittston) at the falls of the Lackawanna river, near here, in the year 1774. In passing down the valley one cannot fail to observe, as he passes over the Lackawanna bridge below the rapids, a deep, ragged, narrow passage cut through the rocks, that here at one time turned aside the waters of the stream as they come fretting and chaffing over the rocky bed. This channel was dug out as early as 1774 for mill purposes, as stated. It was afterwards utilized by Messrs. Smith and Sutton in running their forge. In the early days, owing to the magnificent water power of the Lackawanna, Spring Brook, Ascension, Mill and Keys or Keisers creek, many enterprises sprang up. There were saw and grist mills, forges, bloomers, distilleries, tan yards, foundries, &c. Cornelius Atherton resided at Keys Creek. He was a blacksmith, and it is said that the first clothiers shears in the United States were made by him. Prior to July 8, 1778, a saw mill was erected on the same creek by Timothy Keys. He was killed by Indians on that date. Samuel Miller built a saw mill and a small log grist mill on Mill Creek in 1782. N. Hurlbut erected, at Old Forge, in 1805, a carding machine, the first one erected in the county. Quite a village sprang up in what is now known locally as Drake-town. Old Forge, as a centre, when Luzerne county embraced the counties of Bradford, Lackawanna, Susquehanna and Wyoming, was, without doubt, the busiest place in the county. In this important centre Methodism found a lodgment which showed the keen vision of Father Owen in establishing a class at this point. In 1828 there were but fourteen heads of families living within the present limits of the borough of Pittston, and John Stewart, Sr., the father of the man whose memory we meet to commemorate, was one of these. Wilkes-Barre, in 1795, contained but forty-five dwellings. Old Forge was of so much importance that the second postmaster of Pittston removed his office near here. Anning Owen was the apostle of Methodism in Wyoming. He was one of the hand full of courageous men who were defeated and scattered by an overwhelming force under the command of Colonel John Butler. In the battle and massacre of Wyoming, in 1778, he was by the side of his brother-in-law, Benjamin Carpenter, who afterwards became one of the judges of Luzerne county. He stood the fire of the enemy and answered it shot after shot in such quick succession that the band of his gun became burning hot. "My gun is so hot that I cannot hold it," exclaimed the brave patriot soldier. "Do the best you can then," was the reply of his friend. A shot or two more and the day was lost. Owen and Carpenter fled to the river and secreted themselves under cover of a large grape vine which hung from the branches of a tree and lay in the water. There they laid in safety until the darkness of the night enabled them to gain the fort. They were a portion of the small number who escaped with their lives from the bloody encounter without swimming the river. In the account which Mr. Owen often subsequently gave of his escape he stated that when upon the run he expected every moment to be shot or tomahawked, and the terrible thought of being sent into eternity unprepared filled his soul with horror. He prayed as he ran, and when he lay in the water his every breath was occupied with the silent but earnest prayer, "God have mercy on my soul." There and then it was that he gave his heart to God and vowed to be his forever. Mr. Owen returned to the east with the fugitives, but he was a changed man. He considered his deliverance from death as little short of a miracle, and that in it there was a wise and gracious design which had reference to his eternal well being. He was now a man of prayer, possessed a tender conscience and indulged a trembling hope in Christ. In this condition Mr. Owen became acquainted with the Methodists. Their earnest and powerful preaching and the doctrines which they taught met in his heart a ready response. He was of an ardent temperament and was never in favor of half way measures in anything. He soon drank in the spirit of the early Methodists, and was as full of enthusiasm as any of them. His religious experience became more deep and thorough and his evidence of sins forgiven more clear and satisfactory. He now rejoiced greatly in the liberty wherewith Christ had made him free and panted to be useful. The language of his inmost soul was:

> "O, that the world might taste and see
> The riches of his grace,
> The arms of love that compass me,
> Would all mankind embrace."

In this state of mind Mr. Owen returned to Wyoming and settled among his old companions in tribulation. He was a blacksmith and he commenced, as he supposed, hammering out his fortune in what is now the borough of Dorranceton, at the point where the highway crosses a branch of Toby's Creek. Mr. Owen had no sooner become settled in Wyoming than he commenced conversation with his neighbors upon the subject of religion, and began, with many tears, to tell them what great things God had done for his soul. His words were as coals of fire upon the heads and the hearts of those he addressed, and he soon found that a deep sympathy with his ideas and feelings was abroad, and rapidly extending. He appointed prayer meetings in his own house. The people were melted down under his prayers, his exhortations and singing. He was invited to appoint meetings at other places in the neighborhood, and he listened to the call. A revival of religion broke out at Ross Hill, about a mile from his residence, and just across the line which then separated the townships of Kingston and Plymouth. Great power attended the simple, earnest efforts of the blacksmith, and souls were converted to God. He studied the openings of Providence and tried in all things to follow the Divine light. He was regarded by the young converts as their spiritual father, and to him they looked for advice and comfort. Mr. Owen now considered himself providentially called upon to provide, at least temporally, for the spiritual wants of his flock, and he formed them into a class. Most of the members of the little band resided in the neighborhood of Ross Hill, that point became the center of operations. This class was called the Ross Hill class until the old order of things passed away. It was formed in 1788. The little band was, for the time, well content to regard as their spiritual guide the man who had first raised the standard of the cross in their midst, and being the means under God of their conversion. He had not been constituted in the regular way either preacher, exhorter or class leader, and yet he exercised the functions of all these offices under the sanction of Providence, and to the great satisfaction and edification of the little church in the wilderness. Mr. Owen proceeded for a while under his extraordinary commission but finally began to be seriously exercised in mind upon the subject of the ministry. He visited some point at the east where Methodism had a local habitation and a name, and on returning, at a meeting of his society, said: "I have received a regular license to preach and now have full power to proceed in the work." Among the families connected with Methodism in Wyoming in its infancy, were those of Adams, Baker, Brown, Bidlack, Carver, Carpenter, Coleman, Carey, Catlin, Dana, Davenport, Denison, Gray, Goodwin, Harris, Harvey, Inman, Johnson, Jenkins, Pierce, Parrish, Pugh, Pringle, Ransom, Russel, Sutton, Turner, Wooley, Wadhams, Williams, Waller, Weeks, and many others. Classes were now or had been established at the house of Jonathan Smith in Newport, at the widow Jameson's in Hanover, at Captain John Vaughn's at Old Forge, at the house of ——— Lucas on Ross Hill, and at the widow Coleman's in Plymouth. It will be observed that the Old Forge class was the only one north of Wilkes-Barre at this time. Rev. Nathaniel B. Mills had the honor of being the first Methodist itinerant who found his way over the mountains into the classic vale of Wyoming. This was in 1789, when he traveled Newburg circuit. Rev. Joseph Lovel, who traveled on Newburg circuit in 1790, was the next preacher who visited the valley. At this period there were no conference lines. The "elders" had a certain number of circuits in charge and the preachers attended conference as directed by Bishop Asbury. In 1790 "Thomas Morrell, elder," embraced within his district New York, Elizabeth Town, Long Island, New Rochelle and Newburg. Thomas Morrell was a major in the Revolutionary

War. In the Conference of 1789 he was ordained an elder, and appointed presiding elder. Asbury, in his journal of 1802, says: "Wonders will never cease. Nothing would serve but I must marry Thomas Morrell to a young woman. Such a solitary wedding I suppose has been but seldom seen. Behold father Morrell fifty-five, father Whatcoat, sixty-six, Francis Asbury, fifty-seven, and the ceremony performed solemnly at the solemn hour of ten at night." The next conference held its session in New York, May 26, 1791. At that conference Rev. James Campbell was appointed to Wyoming, and Rev. Robert Cloud was elder. His district embraced Newburg, Wyoming, New York, New Rochelle and Long Island. Mrs. Bedford, who was the daughter of James Sutton, says: "Mr. Campbell preached at my father's once in two weeks. It was like preaching to the walls! Pittston was, at that time, a very hardened place, and great prejudice was raised against us." Thus was the Church established in the wilderness. The same year that regular preaching was held at Old Forge the sainted Wesley died. On Wednesday, May 8, 1792, Rev. William Colbert, in his journal, says: "Road to Lackawanna Forge and preached at James Sutton's on I Cor. 6: 19, 20. Here I met with a disputing calvinist" [probably Dr. Smith]. "Sister Sutton and her daughter" [Mrs. Bedford], "appeared to be very clever women." In 1793 Bishop Asbury visited Wyoming and no doubt preached at Old Forge. In his journal, under date of July 8, he says: "I took the wilderness through the mountains, up the Lackawanna on the twelve mile swamp. This place is famous for dirt and lofty hemlock. We lodged in the middle of the swamp, at S's, and made out better than we expected." In 1807 Bishop Asbury again visited Wyoming. Under date of July 17, he says: "To Sutton's, ten miles; the house neat as a palace, and we were entertained like kings by a king and queen. It was no small consolation to lie down on a clean floor after all we had suffered from dirt and its consequences. Once more I am at Wyoming. We have worried through and clambered over one hundred miles of the rough roads of wild Susquehanna. Oh! the precipitous banks, winding narrows, rocks, sidling hills, obstructive paths, and fords scarcely fordable, ruts, stumps and gulleys." In 1811 he was again at Wyoming. This was probably his last visit to this section of the country. The great body of the early Methodist preachers were plain, uneducated men, who had come immediately from the masses of the people. They were acquainted with the views and feelings of their congregations, and their sermons were adapted to people like themselves. The itinerating system brought them in contact with an immense variety of character, imparting a most valuable knowledge of human nature, while their extensive circuits furnished sufficient of exercise to develop and strengthen the physical powers and to give robust constitutions. They were pious, earnest men, imbued with a deep sense of their responsibility, and with a solemn concern for the souls of their fellow men. They did not confine their ministrations to the highways, and to the densely populated districts, but they penetrated along the by-paths, into the secluded valleys, and among the mountains. They preached in school houses, in private dwellings, in barns, and in the open air, once in every work day in the week, and twice or thrice on Sunday. They went into the new settlements, preached, reached the hearts of their hearers formed classes, enjoined on them to read the word of God, to meet often for prayer, and "Gave out" that at such a time, the Lord willing, they would be along again. Wherever they went the people received them gladly, for, apart from their sacred office, they were a most interesting class of men, who possessed an immense fund of information, gathered in their travels from observation, and from the conversation of others. Still theirs was a life of hardship. The country was a wilderness, the roads were generally in a most wretched condition, and the people were poor. Their annual salary was sixty-four dollars, and traveling expenses, and none but most devout Christians, who looked to a future state of happiness as the only thing worth striving for, could have been so indefatigable in their labors, and so self-sacrificing in their lives. They have left a wonderful monument of their labors and self-denial behind them. On the foundation they laid and on the structure they raised, a vast multitude of busy hands have been engaged, and that grand monument is rising higher and higher towards the heavens, and attracting more and more the attention of mankind. In 1784, at the "Christmas Conference," the Methodist Episcopal Church of the United States was duly organized. She had, at this time, several hundred local preachers, 83 itinerants, of which 63 assisted at the Conference, and 14,988 members. In 1789 she was the first of the religious denominations to send an address of congratulation to General Washington after his introduction into the office of first president of the United States. In 1800 there were 54,894 communicates of Methodist Churches in the United States. In 1890 she had 4,980,240 communicants. Happily there is not the least sign of this tide tending to ebb, and by another centenary of Wesley's death may it not, with other kindred streams, have covered the earth as the waters cover the sea.

www.ingramcontent.com/pod-product-compliance
Lightning Source LLC
Chambersburg PA
CBHW030256170426
43202CB00009B/765